NOUNS.

A Noun is the name of any person, place, or thing, that can be known or mentioned: as, *George, York, man, apple, truth.*

OBSERVATIONS.

OBS. 1.—All words and signs taken *technically*, (that is, independently of their meaning, and merely as things spoken of,) are *nouns*; or, rather, are *things* read and construed *as nouns*; because, in such a use, they temporarily assume the *syntax* of nouns: as, "For this reason, I prefer *contemporary* to *cotemporary.*"—*Campbell's Rhet.*, p. 175; *Murray's Gram.*, i, p. 368. "I and J were formerly expressed by the same character; as were U and V."—*W. Allen's Gram.*, p. 3. "*Us* is a personal pronoun."—*Murray.* "*Th* has two sounds."—*Ib.* "The *'s* cannot be a contraction of *his*, because *'s* is put to *female* [feminine] nouns; as, *Woman's beauty, the Virgin's delicacy.*"—*Dr. Johnson's Gram.* "*Their* and *theirs* are the possessives likewise of *they*, when *they* is the plural of *it.*"—*Ib.* "Let B be a *now* or instant."—*Harris's Hermes*, p. 103. "In such case, I say that the instant B is the end of the time A B."—*Ib.*, 103. "*A* is sometimes a noun: as, a great *A.*"—*Todd's Johnson.* "Formerly *sp* was cast in a piece, as *st's* are now."—*Hist. of Printing*, 1770. "I write to others than he will perhaps include in his *we.*"—*Barclay's Works*, Vol. iii, p. 455. "Here are no fewer than eight *ands* in one sentence."—

Blair's Rhet., p. 112; *Murray's Gram.*, Vol. i, p. 319. "Within this wooden *O*;" i. e., circle.—*Shak.*

OBS. 2.—In parsing, the learner must observe the sense and use of each word, and class it accordingly. Many words commonly belonging to other parts of speech are occasionally used as nouns; and, since it is the manner of its use, that determines any word to be of one part of speech rather than of an other, whatever word is used directly as a noun, must of course be parsed as such.

1. Adjectives made nouns: "The *Ancient* of days did sit."—*Bible.* "Of the *ancients*."—*Swift.* "For such *impertinents*."—*Steele.* "He is an *ignorant* in it."—*Id.* "In the luxuriance of an unbounded *picturesque*."—*Jamieson.* "A source of *the sublime*;" i. e., of sublimity.—*Burke.* "The vast *immense* of space:" i. e., immensity.—*Murray.* "There is none his *like*."—*Job*, xli, 33. "A *little* more than a *little*, is by *much* too *much*."—*Shakspeare.* "And gladly make *much* of that entertainment."—*Sidney.* "A covetous man makes *the most* of what he has."—*L'Estrange.* "It has done *enough* for me."—*Pope.* "He had *enough* to do."—*Bacon.*

"*All* withers here; who *most* possess, are losers by their gain,
Stung by full proof, that bad at best, life's idle *all* is vain."
—*Young.*

"Nor grudge I thee *the much* the Grecians give,
Nor murm'ring take *the little* I receive."
—*Dryden.*

2. Pronouns made nouns: "A love of seeing the *what* and *how* of all about him."—STORY'S LIFE OF FLAXMAN: *Pioneer,* Vol. i, p. 133. "The nameless HE, whose nod is Nature's birth."—*Young*, Night iv. "I was wont to load my *she* with knacks."—*Shak. Winter's Tale.* "Or any *he*, the proudest

English Grammar

- Nouns and Adjectives -

Rodney V. Foster

of thy sort."—*Shak.* "I am the happiest *she* in Kent."—*Steele.* "The *shes* of Italy."—*Shak.* "The *hes* in birds."—*Bacon.* "We should soon have as many *hes* and *shes* as the French."—*Cobbet's E. Gram.*, Para. 42. "If, for instance, we call a nation a *she*, or the sun a *he*."—*Ib.*, Para. 198. "When I see many *its* in a page, I always tremble for the writer."—*Ib.*, Para. 196. "Let those two questionary petitioners try to do this with their *whos* and their *whiches*."—SPECT: *Ash's Gr.*, p. 131.

"Such mortal drugs I have; but Mantua's law
Is death to any *he* that utters them."—*Shak.*

3. Verbs made nouns: "Avaunt all attitude, and *stare*, and *start* theatric."—*Cowper.* "A *may-be* of mercy is sufficient."—*Bridge.* "Which *cuts* are reckoned among the fractures."—*Wiseman.* "The officer erred in granting a *permit*."—"Feel darts and charms, *attracts* and flames."— *Hudibras.* "You may know by the falling off of the *come*, or sprout."— *Mortimer.* "And thou hast talk'd of *sallies* and *retires*."—*Shak.*

"For all that else did come, were sure to fail;
Yet would he further none, but for *avail*."—*Spenser.*

4. Participles made nouns: "For the *producing* of real happiness."— *Crabb.* "For the *crying* of the poor and the *sighing* of the needy, I will arise."—*Bible.* "Surely the *churning* of milk bringeth forth butter, and the *wringing* of the nose bringeth forth blood; so the *forcing* of wrath bringeth forth strife."—*Prov.*, xxx, 33. "*Reading, writing*, and *ciphering*, are indispensable to civilized man."—"Hence was invented the distinction between *doing* and *permitting*."—*Calvin's Inst.*, p. 131. "Knowledge of the *past* comes next."—*Hermes*, p. 113. "I am my *beloved's*, and his desire is toward me."—*Sol. Song*, vii, 10. "Here's—a simple *coming-in* for one man."—*Shak.*

"What are thy rents? What are thy *comings-in*?
O Ceremony, show me but thy worth."—*Id.*

5. Adverbs made nouns: "In these cases we examine the *why*, the *what*, and the *how* of things."—*L'Estrange.* "If a point or *now* were extended, each of them would contain within itself infinite other points or *nows*."—*Hermes*, p. 101. "The *why* is plain as way to parish church."—*Shak.* "'Tis Heaven itself that points out *an hereafter*."—*Addison.* "The dread of *a hereafter*."—*Fuller.* "The murmur of the deep *amen*."—*Sir W. Scott.* "For their *whereabouts* lieth in a mystery."—*Book of Thoughts*, p. 14. Better: "Their *whereabout* lieth," or, "Their *whereabouts* lie," &c.

"Bid them farewell, Cordelia, though unkind;
Thou losest *here*, a better *where* to find."—*Shak.*

6. Conjunctions made nouns: "The *if*, which is here employed, converts the sentence into a supposition."—*Blair's Rhet.* "Your *if* is the only peacemaker; much virtue is in *if*."—*Shak.*

"So his Lordship decreed with a grave solemn tone,
  Decisive and clear, without one *if* or *but*—
That whenever the Nose put his spectacles on,
  By daylight or candlelight—Eyes should be shut."—*Cowper.*

7. Prepositions made nouns: "O, not like me; for mine's beyond *beyond*."—*Shakspeare: Cymb.*, iii, 2. "I. e., her longing is *further than beyond*; beyond any thing that desire can be said to be beyond."—*Singer's Notes.* "You whirled them to the back of *beyont* to look at the auld Roman camp."—*Antiquary*, i. 37.

8. Interjections or phrases made nouns: "Come away from all the *lo-heres*! and *lo-theres*!"—*Sermon.* "Will cuts him short with a '*What*

then?'"—*Addison*. "With *hark* and *whoop*, and wild *halloo*."—*Scott*. "And made a *pish* at chance and sufferance."—*Shak*.

"A single look more marks th' internal wo,
Than all the windings of the lengthen'd *oh*."—*Lloyd*.

CLASSES.

Nouns are divided into two general classes; *proper* and *common*. I. A *proper noun* is the name of some particular individual, or people, or group; as, *Adam, Boston*, the *Hudson*, the *Romans*, the *Azores*, the *Alps*.

II. A *common noun* is the name of a sort, kind, or class, of beings or things; as, *Beast, bird, fish, insect,—creatures, persons, children*.

The particular classes, *collective, abstract*, and *verbal*, or *participial*, are usually included among common nouns. The name of a thing *sui generis* is also called common.

1. A *collective noun*, or *noun of multitude*, is the name of many individuals together; as, *Council, meeting, committee, flock*.

2. An *abstract noun* is the name of some particular quality considered apart from its substance; as, *Goodness, hardness, pride, frailty*.

3. A *verbal* or *participial noun* is the name of some action, or state of being; and is formed from a verb, like a participle, but employed as a noun: as, "The *triumphing* of the wicked is short."—*Job*, xx, 5.

4. A thing *sui generis*, (i. e., *of its own peculiar kind*,) is something which is distinguished, not as an individual of a species, but as a sort by itself,

without plurality in either the noun or the sort of thing; as, *Galvanism, music, geometry.*

OBS. 1.—Through the influence of an article, a proper name sometimes acquires the import of a common noun: as, "He is *the Cicero* of his age;" that is, *the great orator.* "Many *a fiery Alp*;" that is, *high volcanic mountain.* "Such is the following application of famous names; a Solomon for a wise man, a Croesus for a rich man, a Judas for a traitor, a Demosthenes for an orator, and a Homer for a poet."—*Campbell's Rhet.,* p. 326.

"Consideration, like an angel, came,
And whipp'd *th' offending Adam* out of him."—*Shak.*

OBS. 2.—A common noun, with the definite article before it, sometimes becomes proper: as, *The Park; the Strand; the Gharmel; the Downs; the United States.*

OBS. 3.—The common name of a thing or quality personified, often becomes proper; our conception of the object being changed by the figure of speech: as, "My power," said *Reason,* "is to advise, not to compel."—*Johnson.* "Fair *Peace* her olive branch extends." For such a word, the form of parsing should be like this: "*Peace* is a *common noun, personified proper*; of the third person, singular number, feminine gender, and nominative case." Here the construction of the word as a proper noun, and of the *feminine gender,* is the result of the personification, and contrary to the literal usage.

MODIFICATIONS.

Nouns have modifications of four kinds; namely, *Persons, Numbers, Genders,* and *Cases.*

PERSONS.

Persons, in grammar, are modifications that distinguish the speaker, the hearer, and the person or thing merely spoken of.

There are three persons; the *first*, the *second*, and the *third*.

The *first person* is that which denotes the speaker or writer; as, "*I Paul* have written it."

The second person is that which denotes the hearer, or the person addressed; as, "*Robert*, who did this?"

The third person is that which denotes the person or thing merely spoken of; as, "*James* loves his book."

OBSERVATIONS.

OBS. 1.—The distinction of persons is founded on the different relations which the objects mentioned in any discourse may bear to the discourse itself. The speaker or writer, being the mover and maker of the communication, of course stands in the nearest or *first* of these relations. The hearer or hearers, being personally present and directly addressed, evidently sustain the next or *second* of these relations; this relation is also that of the reader, when he peruses what is addressed to himself in print or writing. Lastly, whatsoever or whosoever is merely mentioned in the discourse, bears to it that more remote relation which constitutes the *third* person. The distinction of persons belongs to nouns, pronouns, and finite verbs; and to these it is always applied, either by peculiarity of form or construction, or by inference from the principles of concord. Pronouns are like their antecedents, and verbs are like their subjects, in person.

OBS. 2.—Of the persons, numbers, genders, cases, and some other grammatical modifications of words, it should be observed that they belong not exclusively to any one part of speech, but jointly and equally, to two or three. Hence, it is necessary that our *definitions* of these things be such as will apply to each of them in full, or under all circumstances; for the definitions ought to be as general in their application as are the things or properties defined. Any person, number, gender, case, or other grammatical modification, is really but one and the same thing, in whatever part of speech it may be found. This is plainly implied in the very nature of every form of syntactical agreement; and as plainly contradicted in one half, and probably more, of the definitions usually given of these things.

OBS. 3.—Let it be understood, that *persons, in grammar,* are not *words,* but mere forms, relations, or modifications of words; that they are things, thus named by a *figure*; *things* of the neuter gender, and not living souls. But persons, in common parlance, or in ordinary life, are *intelligent beings,* of one or the other sex. These objects, different as they are in their nature, are continually confounded by the makers of English grammars: as, "The *first* person is *the person who speaks.*"—*Comly's Gram.*, p. 17. So Bicknell, of London: "The *first person* speaks of *himself*; as, *I John take thee Elizabeth.* The *second* person has the speech directed to *him,* and is supposed to be present; as, *Thou Harry art a wicked fellow.* The *third* person is spoken of, or described, and supposed to be *absent*; as, *That Thomas is a good man.* And in the same manner the plural pronouns are used, when more than one are spoken of."—*Bicknell's Grammatical Wreath*, p. 50. "The person speaking is the first person; the person spoken to, the second; and the person spoken of, the third."—*Russell's Gram.*, p. 16. "The first person is the speaker."—*Parker & Fox's Gram.*, Part i, p. 6. "Person is that, which distinguishes a noun, that speaks, one spoken to, or one spoken about."—*S. B. Hall's Gram.*, p. 6. "A noun that speaks!" A noun "spoken to!" If ever one of Father Hall's nouns shall speak for itself, or answer when "spoken to," will it not reprove him? And how can the *first person* be "the *person* WHO *speaks*," when every word of this phrase is of the *third* person? Most certainly, *it is not* HE, nor any one of his sort. If any body can boast of being "*the first person in grammar*," I pray, *Who* is it? Is it not *I*, even *I*? Many grammarians say so. But nay: such authors know not what the first person in grammar is. The Rev. Charles Adams, with infinite absurdity, makes the three persons in grammar to be never any thing but *three nouns*, which hold a confabulation thus: "Person is defined to be *that* which distinguishes a *noun that speaks, one spoken to, or one spoken of.* The *noun* that speaks [,] is the first person; as, *I, James,* was present. The *noun* that is spoken to, is the second person; as, *James,* were you present? The *noun* that is spoken of is the third person; as, *James* was present."—*Adams's System of English Gram.*, p. 9. What can be a greater blunder, than to call the first person of a verb, of a pronoun, or even of a noun, "*the noun that speaks?*" What can be more absurd than are the following assertions? "*Nouns* are *in* the first person when *speaking. Nouns* are *of* the second person when *addressed* or *spoken to.*"—*O. C. Felton's Gram.*, p. 9.

OBS. 4.—An other error, scarcely less gross than that which has just been noticed, is the very common one of identifying the three grammatical persons with certain *words*, called personal pronouns: as, "*I* is the first person, *thou* the second, *he, she* or *it,* the third."—*Smith's Productive Gram.*, p. 53. "*I* is the first person, singular. *Thou* is the second person, singular. *He, she,* or *it,* is the third person, singular. *We* is the first person, plural. *Ye* or *you* is the second person, plural. *They* is the third person, plural."—*L. Murray's Grammar*, p. 51; *Ingersoll's*, 54; *D. Adams's*, 37; *A. Flint's*, 18; *Kirkham's*, 98; *Cooper's*, 34; *T. H. Miller's*, 26; *Hull's*, 21; *Frost's*, 13; *Wilcox's*, 18; *Bacon's*, 19; *Alger's*, 22; *Maltby's*, 19; *Perley's*, 15; *S. Putnam's*, 22. Now there is no more propriety in affirming, that "*I is the first person,*" than in declaring that *me, we, us, am, ourselves, we think, I write,* or any other word or phrase *of* the first person, *is* the first person.

Yet Murray has given us no other definitions or explanations of the persons than the foregoing erroneous assertions; and, if I mistake not, all the rest who are here named, have been content to define them only as he did. Some others, however, have done still worse: as, "There are *three* personal pronouns; so called, because they denote the three persons, *who* are the subjects of a discourse, viz. 1st. *I, who is* the person *speaking*; 2d *thou, who is* spoken to; 3d *he, she,* or *it, who* is spoken of, and their plurals, *we, ye* or *you, they.*"—*Bingham's Accidence*, 20th Ed., p. 7. Here the two kinds of error which I have just pointed out, are jumbled together. It is impossible to write *worse English* than this! Nor is the following much better: "Of the personal pronouns there are five, viz. *I,* in the first person, speaking; *Thou,* in the second person, spoken to; and *He, she, it,* in the third person, spoken of."—*Nutting's Gram.*, p. 25.

OBS. 5.—In *written* language, the *first person* denotes the writer or author; and the *second,* the reader or person addressed: except when the writer describes not himself, but some one else, as uttering to an other the words which he records. This exception takes place more particularly in the writing of dialogues and dramas; in which the first and second persons are abundantly used, not as the representatives of the author and his reader, but as denoting the fictitious speakers and hearers that figure in each scene. But, in discourse, the grammatical persons may be changed without a change of the living subject. In the following sentence, the three grammatical persons are all of them used with reference to one and the same individual: "Say ye of *Him whom* the Father hath sanctified and sent into the world, *Thou blasphemest,* because *I said I am* the *Son* of *God?*"—*John,* x, 36.

OBS. 6.-The speaker seldom refers to himself *by name,* as the speaker; and, of the objects which there is occasion to name in discourse, but comparatively few are such as can ever be supposed to speak.

Consequently, *nouns* are rarely used in the first person; and when they do assume this relation, a pronoun is commonly associated with them: as, "*I John*,"—"*We Britons*." These words I conceive to agree throughout, in person, number, gender, and case; though it must be confessed, that agreement like this is not always required between words in apposition. But some grammarians deny the first person to nouns altogether; others, with much more consistency, ascribe it;[140] while very many are entirely silent on the subject. Yet it is plain that both the doctrine of concords, and the analogy of general grammar, require its admission. The reason of this may be seen in the following examples: "*Themistocles ad te veni.*" "I Themistocles have come to you."—*Grant's Latin Gram.*, p. 72. "*Adsum Troius Æneas.*"—*Virgil.* "*Romulus Rex regia arma offero.*"—Livy. "*Annibal peto pacem.*"—Id. "*Callopius recensui.*"—See *Terence's Comedies, at the end.* "*Paul*, an apostle, &c., unto Timothy, *my* own son in the faith."—*1 Tim.*, i, 2. Again, if the word *God* is of the second person, in the text, "*Thou, God*, seest me," why should any one deny that *Paul* is of the first person, in this one? "*I Paul* have written it."—*Philemon*, 19. Or this? "The salutation by the hand of *me Paul.*"—*Col.*, iv, 18. And so of the plural: "Of *you builders.*"—*Acts*, iv, 11. "Of *us the apostles.*"—*2 Pet.*, iii, 2. How can it be pretended, that, in the phrase, "*I Paul*," *I* is of the first person, as denoting the speaker, and *Paul*, of some other person, as denoting something or somebody that is *not* the speaker? Let the admirers of Murray, Kirkham, Ingersoll, R. C. Smith, Comly, Greenleaf, Parkhurst, or of any others who teach this absurdity, answer.

OBS. 7.—As, in the direct application of what are called Christian names, there is a kind of familiarity, which on many occasions would seem to indicate a lack of proper respect; so in a frequent and familiar use of the second person, as it is the placing of an other in the more intimate relation of the hearer, and one's self in that of the speaker, there is a sort of assumption which may seem less modest and respectful than to use the third person. In the following example, the patriarch Jacob uses both forms; applying the term *servant* to himself, and to his brother Esau the term *lord*: "Let *my lord, I* pray *thee*, pass over before *his servant*: and *I* will lead on softly."—*Gen.*, xxxiii, 14. For when a speaker or writer does not choose to declare himself in the *first* person, or to address his hearer or reader in the *second*, he speaks of both or either in the *third*. Thus Moses relates what *Moses* did, and Cæsar records the achievements of *Cæsar*. So Judah humbly beseeches Joseph: "Let *thy servant* abide in stead of the lad a bondman to *my lord*."—*Gen.*, xliv, 33. And Abraham reverently intercedes with God: "Oh! let not *the Lord* be angry, and I will speak."—*Gen.*, xviii, 30. And the Psalmist prays: "*God* be merciful unto us, and bless us; and cause *his* face to shine upon us."—*Ps.*, lxvii, 1. So, on more common occasions:—

"As will the rest, so *willeth Winchester*."—*Shak.*

"Richard of York, how *fares* our dearest *brother*?"—*Id.*[141]

OBS. 8.—When inanimate things are spoken to, they are *personified*; and their names are put in the second person, because by the figure the objects are *supposed* to be capable of hearing: as, "What ailed thee, *O thou sea*, that thou fleddest? *thou Jordan*, that thou wast driven back? *Ye mountains*, that ye skipped like rams; and *ye little hills*, like lambs? Tremble, *thou earth*, at the presence of the Lord, at the presence of the God of Jacob."—*Psalms*, cxiv, 5-7.

NUMBERS.

Numbers, in grammar, are modifications that distinguish unity and plurality.

There are two numbers; the *singular* and the *plural*.

The *singular number* is that which denotes but one; as, "The *boy learns*."

The *plural number* is that which denotes more than one; as, "The *boys learn*."

The plural number *of nouns* is regularly formed by adding *s* or *es* to the singular: as, *book, books; box, boxes; sofa, sofas; hero, heroes*.

When the singular ends in a sound which will unite with that of *s*, the plural is generally formed by adding *s only*, and the number of syllables is not increased: as, *pen, pens; grape, grapes*.

But when the sound of *s* cannot be united with that of the primitive word, the regular plural adds *s* to final *e*, and *es* to other terminations, and forms a separate syllable: as, *page, pages; fox, foxes*.

OBSERVATIONS.

OBS. 1.—The distinction of numbers serves merely to show whether we speak of one object, or of more. In some languages, as the Greek and the Arabic, there is a *dual* number, which denotes *two*, or a *pair*; but in ours, this property of words, or class of modifications, extends no farther than to distinguish unity from plurality, and plurality from unity. It belongs to nouns, pronouns, and finite verbs; and to these it is always applied, either by peculiarity of form, or by inference from the principles of concord. Pronouns are like their antecedents, and verbs are like their subjects, in number.

OBS. 2.—The most common way of forming the plural of English nouns, is that of simply adding to them an *s*; which, when it unites with a sharp consonant, is always sharp, or hissing; and when it follows a vowel or a flat mute, is generally flat, like *z*: thus, in the words, *ships, skiffs, pits, rocks, depths, lakes, gulfs*, it is sharp; but in *seas, lays, rivers, hills, ponds, paths, rows, webs, flags*, it is flat. The terminations which always make the regular plural in *es*, with increase of syllables, are twelve; namely, *ce, ge, ch* soft, *che* soft, *sh, ss, s, se, x, xe, z*, and *ze*: as in *face, faces; age, ages; torch, torches; niche, niches; dish, dishes; kiss, kisses; rebus, rebuses; lens, lenses; chaise, chaises; corpse, corpses; nurse, nurses; box, boxes; axe, axes; phiz, phizzes; maze, mazes.* All other endings readily unite in sound either with the sharp or with the flat *s*, as they themselves are sharp or flat; and, to avoid an increase of syllables, we allow the final *e* mute to remain mute after that letter is added: thus, we always pronounce as monosyllables the words *babes, blades, strifes, tithes, yokes, scales, names, canes, ropes, shores, plates, doves*, and the like.

OBS. 3.—Though the irregular plurals of our language appear considerably numerous when brought together, they are in fact very few in comparison with the many thousands that are perfectly simple and regular. In some instances, however, usage is various in writing, though uniform in speech; an unsettlement peculiar to certain words that terminate in vowels: as, *Rabbis*, or *rabbies; octavos*, or *octavoes; attornies*, or *attorneys*. There are also some other difficulties respecting the plurals of nouns, and especially respecting those of foreign words; of compound terms; of names and titles; and of words redundant or deficient in regard to the numbers. What is most worthy of notice, respecting all these puzzling points of English grammar, is briefly contained in the following observations.

OBS. 4.—It is a general rule of English grammar, that all singular nouns ending with a vowel preceded by an other vowel, shall form the plural by simply assuming an *s*: as, *Plea, pleas; idea, ideas; hernia, hernias; bee, bees; lie, lies; foe, foes; shoe, shoes; cue, cues; eye, eyes; folio, folios; bamboo, bamboos; cuckoo, cuckoos; embryo, embryos; bureau, bureaus; purlieu, purlieus; sou, sous; view, views; straw, straws; play, plays; key, keys; medley, medleys; viceroy, viceroys; guy, guys.* To this rule, the plurals of words ending in *quy*, as *alloquies, colloquies, obloquies, soliloquies*, are commonly made exceptions; because many have conceived that the *u*, in such instances, is a mere appendage to the *q*, or is a consonant having the power of *w*, and not a vowel forming a diphthong with the *y*. All other deviations from the rule, as *monies* for *moneys, allies* for *alleys, vallies* for *valleys, chimnies* for *chimneys,* &c., are now usually condemned as errors. See Rule 12th for Spelling.

OBS. 5.—It is also a general principle, that nouns ending in *y* preceded by a consonant, change the *y* into *i*, and add *es* for the plural, without increase of syllables: as, *fly, flies; ally, allies; city, cities; colony, colonies.* So nouns in *i*, (so far as we have any that are susceptible of a change of number,) form the plural regularly by assuming *es*: as, *alkali, alkalies; salmagundi, salinagundies.* Common nouns ending in *y* preceded by a consonant, are numerous; and none of them deviate from the foregoing rule of forming the plural: thus, *duty, duties.* The termination added is *es*, and the *y* is changed into *i*, according to the general principle expressed in Rule 11th for Spelling. But, to this principle, or rule, some writers have supposed that *proper nouns* were to be accounted exceptions. And accordingly we sometimes find such names made plural by the mere addition of an *s*; as, "How come the *Pythagoras',* [it should be, *the Pythagorases*,] the *Aristotles,* the *Tullys,* the *Livys,* to appear, even to us at this distance, as stars of the first magnitude in the vast fields of ether?"—*Burgh's Dignity,* Vol. i, p. 131. This doctrine, adopted from some of our older grammars, I was myself, at one period, inclined to countenance; (see *Institutes of English Grammar*, p. 33, at the bottom;) but further observation having led me to suspect, there is more *authority* for changing the *y* than for retaining it, I shall by-and-by exhibit some examples of this change, and leave the reader to take his choice of the two forms, or principles.

OBS. 6.—The vowel *a*, at the end of a word, (except in the questionable term *huzza*, or when silent, as in *guinea*,) has always its Italian or middle sound, as heard in the interjection *aha!* a sound which readily unites with that of *s* flat, and which ought, in deliberate speech, to be carefully preserved in plurals from this ending: as, *Canada, the Canadas; cupola, cupolas; comma, commas; anathema, anathemas.* To pronounce the final *a* flat, as *Africay* for *Africa*, is a mark of vulgar ignorance.

OBS. 7.—The vowel *e* at the end of a word, is generally silent; and, even when otherwise, it remains single in plurals from this ending; the *es*, whenever the *e* is vocal, being sounded *eez*, or like the word *ease*: as, *apostrophe, apostrophes; epitome, epitomes; simile, similes.* This class of words being anomalous in respect to pronunciation, some authors have attempted to reform them, by changing the *e* to *y* in the singular, and writing *ies* for the plural: as, *apostrophy, apostrophies; epitomy, epitomies; simily, similies.* A reformation of some sort seems desirable here, and this has the advantage of being first proposed; but it is not extensively adopted, and perhaps never will be; for the vowel sound in question, is not exactly that of the terminations *y* and *ies*, but one which seems to require *ee*—a stronger sound than that of *y*, though similar to it.

OBS. 8.—For nouns ending in open *o* preceded by a consonant, the regular method of forming the plural seems to be that of adding *es*; as in *bilboes, umboes, buboes, calicoes, moriscoes, gambadoes, barricadoes, fumadoes, carbonadoes, tornadoes, bravadoes, torpedoes, innuendoes, viragoes, mangoes, embargoes, cargoes, potargoes, echoes, buffaloes, volcanoes, heroes, negroes, potatoes, manifestoes, mulattoes, stilettoes, woes.* In words of this class, the *e* appears to be useful as a means of preserving the right sound of the *o*; consequently, such of them as are the most frequently used, have become the most firmly fixed in this orthography. In practice, however, we find many similar nouns very frequently, if not uniformly, written with *s* only; as, *cantos, juntos, grottos, solos, quartos, octavos, duodecimos, tyros.* So that even the best scholars seem to have frequently doubted which termination they ought to regard as the *regular* one. The whole class includes more than one hundred words. Some, however, are seldom used in the plural; and others, never. *Wo* and *potato* are sometimes written *woe* and *potatoe*. This may have sprung from a notion, that such as have the *e* in the plural, should have it also in the singular. But this principle has never been carried out; and, being repugnant to derivation, it probably never will be. The only English appellatives that are established in *oe*, are the following fourteen: seven monosyllables, *doe, foe, roe, shoe, sloe, soe, toe*; and seven longer words, *rockdoe, aloe, felloe, canoe, misletoe, tiptoe, diploe*. The last is pronounced *dip'-lo-e* by Worcester; but Webster, Bolles, and some others, give it as a word of two syllables only.[142]

OBS. 9.—Established exceptions ought to be enumerated and treated as exceptions; but it is impossible to remember how to write some scores of words, so nearly alike as *fumadoes* and *grenados*, *stilettoes* and *palmettos*, if they are allowed to differ in termination, as these examples do in Johnson's Dictionary. Nay, for lack of a rule to guide his pen, even Johnson himself could not remember the orthography of the common word *mangoes* well enough to *copy* it twice without inconsistency. This may be seen by his example from King, under the words *mango* and *potargo*. Since, therefore, either termination is preferable to the uncertainty which must attend a division of this class of words between the two; and since *es* has some claim to the preference, as being a better index to the sound; I shall make no exceptions to the principle, that common nouns ending in *o* preceded by a consonant take *es* for the plural. Murray says, "*Nouns which* end in *o* have sometimes *es* added, to form the plural; as, cargo, echo, hero, negro, manifesto, potato, volcano, wo: and sometimes only *s*; as, folio, nuncio, punctilio, seraglio."—*Octavo Gram.*, p. 40. This amounts to nothing, unless it is to be inferred from his *examples*, that others like them in form are to take *s* or *es* accordingly; and this is what I teach, though it cannot be said that Murray maintains the principle.

OBS. 10.—Proper names of *individuals,* strictly used as such, have no plural. But when several persons of the same name are spoken of, the noun becomes in some degree common, and admits of the plural form and an article; as, "*The Stuarts, the Cæsars.*"—*W. Allen's Gram.*, p. 41. These, however, may still be called *proper nouns,* in parsing; because they are only inflections, peculiarly applied, of certain names which are indisputably such. So likewise when such nouns are used to denote character: as, "*Solomons,* for wise men; *Neros,* for tyrants."—*Ib.* "Here we see it becomes a doubt which of the two *Herculeses,* was the monster-queller."—*Notes to Pope's Dunciad*, iv, 492. The proper names of *nations, tribes*, and *societies*, are generally plural; and, except in a direct address, they are usually construed with the definite article: as, "*The Greeks, the Athenians, the Jews, the Jesuits.*" But such words may take the singular form with the indefinite article, as often as we have occasion to speak of an individual of such a people; as, "*A Greek, an Athenian, a Jew, a Jesuit.*" These, too, may be called *proper nouns*; because they are national, patrial, or tribal names, each referring to some place or people, and are not appellatives, which refer to actual sorts or kinds, not considered local.

OBS. 11.—Proper names, when they form the plural, for the most part form it regularly, by assuming *s* or *es* according to the termination: as, *Carolina,* the *Carolinas*; *James,* the *Jameses.* And those which are only or chiefly plural, have, or ought to have, such terminations as are proper to distinguish them as plurals, so that the form for the singular may be inferred: as, "The *Tungooses* occupy nearly a third of Siberia."—*Balbi's Geog.*, p. 379. Here the singular must certainly be *a Tungoose.* "The principal tribes are the *Pawnees,* the *Arrapahoes,* and the *Cumanches,* who roam through the regions of the Platte, the Arkansaw, and the Norte."—*Ib.,*

p. 179. Here the singulars may be supposed to be a *Pawnee*, an *Arrapaho*, and a *Cumanche*. "The Southern or Floridian family comprised the *Cherokees, Creeks, Chickasaws, Choctaws, Seminoles*, and *Natchez*."—*Ib.*, p. 179. Here all are regular plurals, except the last; and this probably ought to be *Natchezes*, but Jefferson spells it *Natches*, the singular of which I do not know. Sometimes foreign words or foreign terminations have been improperly preferred to our own; which last are more intelligible, and therefore better: as, *Esquimaux*, to *Esquimaus*; *Knistenaux*, to *Knistenaus*, or *Crees*; *Sioux*, to *Sious*, or *Dahcotahs*; *Iroquois*, to *Iroquoys*, or *Hurons*.

OBS. 12.—Respecting the plural of nouns ending in *i, o, u,* or *y*, preceded by a consonant, there is in present usage much uncertainty. As any vowel sound may be uttered with an *s*, many writers suppose these letters to require for plurals strictly regular, the *s* only; and to take *es* occasionally, by way of exception. Others, (perhaps with more reason,) assume, that the most usual, regular, and proper endings for the plural, in these instances, are *ies, oes, and ues*: as, *alkali, alkalies; halo, haloes; gnu, gnues; enemy, enemies*. This, I think, is right for common nouns. How far proper names are to be made exceptions, because they are proper names, is an other question. It is certain that some of them are not to be excepted: as, for instance, *Alleghany*, the *Alleghanies*; *Sicily*, the Two *Sicilies*; *Ptolemy*, the *Ptolemies*; *Jehu*, the *Jehues*. So the names of tribes; as, The *Missouries*, the *Otoes*, the *Winnebagoes*. Likewise, the *houries* and the *harpies*; which words, though not strictly proper names, are often written with a capital as such. Like these are *rabbies, cadies, mufties, sophies*, from which some writers omit the *e*. Johnson, Walker, and others, write *gipsy* and *gipsies*; Webster, now writes *Gipsey* and *Gipseys*; Worcester prefers *Gypsy*, and probably *Gypsies*: Webster once wrote the plural *gypsies*; (see his *Essays*, p. 333;) and Johnson cites the following line:—

"I, near yon stile, three sallow *gypsies* met."—*Gay*.

OBS. 13.—Proper names in *o* are commonly made plural by *s* only. Yet there seems to be the same reason for inserting the *e* in these, as in other nouns of the same ending; namely, to prevent the *o* from acquiring a short sound. "I apprehend," says Churchill, "it has been from an erroneous notion of proper names being unchangeable, that some, feeling the necessity of obviating this mispronunciation, have put an apostrophe between the *o* and the *s* in the plural, *in stead of an e*; writing *Cato's, Nero's*; and on a similar principle, *Ajax's, Venus's*; thus using the possessive case singular for the nominative or objective plural. Harris says very properly, 'We have our *Marks* and our *Antonies*: *Hermes*, B. 2, Ch. 4; for which those would have given us *Mark's* and *Antony's*."—*New Gram.*, p. 206. Whatever may have been the motive for it, such a use of the apostrophe is a gross impropriety. "In this quotation, ['From the Socrates's, the Plato's, and the Confucius's of the age,'] the proper names should have been pluralized like common nouns; thus, From the *Socrateses*, the *Platoes*, and the *Confuciuses* of the age."—*Lennie's Gram.*, p. 126; *Bullions's*, 142.

OBS. 14.—The following are some examples of the plurals of proper names, which I submit to the judgement of the reader, in connexion with the foregoing observations: "The Romans had their plurals *Marci* and *Antonii*, as we in later days have our *Marks* and our *Anthonies*."—*Harris's Hermes*, p. 40. "There seems to be more reason for such plurals, as the *Ptolemies*, *Scipios, Catos*: or, to instance in more modern names, the *Howards*, *Pelhams, and Montagues*."—*Ib.*, 40. "Near the family seat of the *Montgomeries* of Coil's-field."—*Burns's Poems*, Note, p. 7. "Tryphon, a surname of one of the *Ptolemies*."—*Lempriere's Dict.* "Sixteen of the *Tuberos*, with their wives and children, lived in a small house."—*Ib.* "What are the *Jupiters* and *Junos* of the heathens to such a God?"—*Burgh's Dignity*, i, 234. "Also when we speak of more than one person of the same name; as, the *Henries*, the *Edwards*."—*Cobbetts E. Gram.*, ¶ 40. "She was descended from the *Percies* and the *Stanleys*."—*Loves of the Poets*, ii, 102.

"Naples, or the *Two Sicilies*."—*Balbi's Geog.*, p. 273. The word *India*, commonly makes the plural *Indies*, not *Indias*; and, for *Ajaxes*, the poets write *Ajaces*. But Richard Hiley says, "Proper nouns, when pluralized, follow the same rules as common nouns; as, Venus, the *Venuses*; Ajax, the *Ajaxes*; Cato, the *Catoes*; Henry, the *Henries*."—*Hiley's E. Gram.*, p. 18.

"He ev'ry day from King to King can walk,
Of all our *Harries*, all our Edwards talk."—*Pope's Satires*, iv.

OBS. 15.—When a name and a title are to be used together in a plural sense, many persons are puzzled to determine whether the name, or the title, or both, should be in the plural form. For example—in speaking of two young ladies whose family name is Bell—whether to call them the *Miss Bells*, the *Misses Bell*, or the *Misses Bells*. To an inquiry on this point, a learned editor, who prefers the last, lately gave his answer thus: "There are two young ladies; of course they are 'the Misses.' Their name is Bell; of course there are two 'Bells.' Ergo, the correct phrase, in speaking of them, is —'the Misses Bells.'"—*N. Y. Com. Adv.* This puts the words in apposition; and there is no question, that it is *formally* correct. But still it is less agreeable to the ear, less frequently heard, and less approved by grammarians, than the first phrase; which, if we may be allowed to assume that the two words may be taken together as a sort of compound, is correct also. Dr. Priestley says, "When a name has a title prefixed to it, as *Doctor, Miss, Master*, &c., the plural termination affects only the latter of the two words; as, 'The two *Doctor Nettletons*'—'The two *Miss Thomsons*;' though a strict analogy would plead for the alteration of the former word, and lead us to say, 'The two *Doctors Nettleton*'—'The two *Misses Thomson*.'"—*Priestley's Gram.*, p. 59. The following quotations show the opinions of some other grammarians: "Two or more nouns in concordance, and forming one complex name, or a name and a title, have the plural termination annexed to the last only; as, 'The *Miss Smiths*'—'The three *Doctor*

Simpsons'—'The two *Master Wigginses*.' With a few exceptions, and those not parallel to the examples just given, we almost uniformly, in complex names, confine the inflection to the last or the latter noun."—*Dr. Crombie.* The foregoing opinion from Crombie, is quoted and seconded by Maunder, who adds the following examples: "Thus, Dr. Watts: 'May there not be *Sir Isaac Newtons* in every science?'—'You must not suppose that the world is made up of *Lady Aurora Granvilles.*'"—*Maunder's Gram.*, p. 2.

OBS. 16.—These writers do not seem to accord with W. L. Stone, the editor above quoted, nor would his reasoning apply well to several of their examples. Yet both opinions are right, if neither be carried too far. For when the words are in apposition, rather than in composition, the first name or title must be made plural, if it refers to more than one: as, "The *Misses Bell and Brown*,"—"*Messrs. Lambert and Son*,"—"The *Lords Calthorpe and Erskine*,"—"The *Lords Bishops* of Durham and St. David's,"—"The *Knights Hospitalers*,"—"The *Knights Templars*,"—"The *Knights Baronets*." But this does not prove the other construction, which varies the last word only, to be irregular; and, if it did, there is abundant authority for it. Nor is that which varies the first only, to be altogether condemned, though Dr. Priestley is unquestionably wrong respecting the "*strict analogy*" of which he speaks. The joining of a plural title to one singular noun, as, "*Misses Roy*,"—"*The Misses Bell*,"—"*The two Misses Thomson*," produces a phrase which is in itself the *least analogous* of the three; but, "*The Misses Jane and Eliza Bell*," is a phrase which nobody perhaps will undertake to amend. It appears, then, that each of these forms of expression may be right in some cases; and each of them may be wrong, if improperly substituted for either of the others.

OBS. 17.—The following statements, though erroneous in several particulars, will show the opinions of some other grammarians, upon the foregoing point: "Proper nouns have the plural only when they refer to a race or family; as, *The Campbells*; or to several persons of the same name; as, *The eight Henrys; the two Mr. Sells; the two Miss Browns*; or, without the numeral, *the Miss Roys*. But in addressing letters in which both or all are equally concerned, and also when the names are different, we pluralize the *title*, (Mr. or Miss,) and write, *Misses* Brown; *Misses* Roy; *Messrs*, (for Messieurs, Fr.) Guthrie and Tait."—*Lennie's Gram.*, p. 7. "If we wish to distinguish the *unmarried* from the *married* Howards, we call them *the Miss Howards*. If we wish to distinguish these Misses from other Misses, we call them the *Misses Howard*."—*Fowle's Gram.* "To distinguish several persons of the same name and family from others of a different name and family, the *title*, and not the *proper name*, is varied to express the distinction; as, the *Misses* Story, the *Messrs.* Story. The elliptical meaning is, the Misses and Messrs, *who are named* Story. To distinguish *unmarried* from *married* ladies, *the proper name*, and not the *title*, should be varied; as, the *Miss* Clarks. When we mention more than one person of different names, the title should be expressed before each; as, *Miss* Burns, *Miss* Parker, and *Miss* Hopkinson, were present."—*Sanborn's Gram.*, p. 79. In the following examples from Pope's Works, the last word only is varied: "He paragons himself to two *Lord Chancellors* for law."—Vol. iii, p. 61. "Yearly panegyrics upon the *Lord Mayors*."—*Ib.*, p. 83.

"Whence hapless Monsieur much complains at Paris
Of wrongs from Duchesses and *Lady Maries*."—*Dunciad*, B. ii, L 135.

OBS. 18.—The following eleven nouns in *f*, change the *f* into *v* and assume *es* for the plural: *sheaf, sheaves; leaf, leaves; loaf, loaves; leaf, beeves; thief, thieves; calf, calves; half, halves; elf, elves; shelf, shelves;*

self, selves; wolf, wolves. Three others in *fe* are similar: *life, lives; knife, knives; wife, wives.* These are specific exceptions to the general rule for plurals, and not a series of examples coming under a particular rule; for, contrary to the instructions of nearly all our grammarians, there are more than twice as many words of the same endings, which take *s* only: as, *chiefs, kerchiefs, handkerchiefs, mischiefs, beliefs, misbeliefs, reliefs, bassreliefs, briefs, feifs, griefs, clefs, semibrefs, oafs, waifs, coifs, gulfs, hoofs, roofs, proofs, reproofs, woofs, califs, turfs, scarfs, dwarfs, wharfs, fifes, strifes, safes.* The plural of *wharf* is sometimes written *wharves*; but perhaps as frequently, and, if so, more accurately, *wharfs.* Examples and authorities: "*Wharf, wharfs.*"—*Brightland's Gram.*, p. 80; *Ward's*, 24; *Goar's*, 26; *Lennie's*, 7; *Bucke's*, 39. "There were not in London so many *wharfs*, or *keys*, for the landing of merchants' goods."—CHILD: *in Johnson's Dict.* "The *wharfs* of Boston are also worthy of notice."—*Balbi's Geog.*, p. 37. "Between banks thickly clad with dwelling-houses, manufactories, and *wharfs.*"—*London Morn. Chronicle*, 1833. Nouns in *ff* take *s* only; as, *skiffs, stuffs, gaffs.* But the plural of *staff* has hitherto been generally written *staves*; a puzzling and useless anomaly, both in form and sound: for all the compounds of *staff* are regular; as, *distaffs, whipstaffs, tipstaffs, flagstaffs, quarterstaffs*; and *staves* is the regular plural of *stave*, a word now in very common use with a different meaning, as every cooper and every musician knows. *Staffs* is now sometimes used; as, "I saw the husbandmen bending over their *staffs.*"—*Lord Carnarvon.* "With their *staffs* in their hands for very age."—*Hope of Israel*, p. 16. "To distinguish between the two *staffs.*"—*Comstock's Elocution*, p. 43. In one instance, I observe, a very excellent scholar has written *selfs* for *selves*, but the latter is the established plural of *self*:

"Self-love would cease, or be dilated, when
We should behold as many *selfs* as men."—*Waller's Poems*, p. 55.

OBS. 19.—Of nouns purely English, the following thirteen are the only simple words that form distinct plurals not ending in *s* or *es*, and four of these are often regular: *man, men; woman, women; child, children; brother, brethren* or *brothers; ox, oxen; goose, geese; foot, feet; tooth, teeth; louse, lice; mouse, mice; die, dice* or *dies; penny, pence* or *pennies; pea, pease* or *peas.* The word *brethren* is now applied only to fellow-members of the same church or fraternity; for sons of the same parents we always use *brothers*; and this form is sometimes employed in the other sense. *Dice* are spotted cubes for gaming; *dies* are stamps for coining money, or for impressing metals. *Pence*, as *six pence*, refers to the amount of money in value; *pennies* denotes the corns themselves. "We write *peas*, for two or more individual seeds; but *pease*, for an indefinite number in quantity or bulk."—*Webster's Dict.* This last anomaly, I think, might well enough "be spared; the sound of the word being the same, and the distinction to the eye not always regarded." Why is it not as proper, to write an order for "a bushel of *peas*," as for "a bushel of *beans*?" "*Peas* and *beans* may be severed from the ground before they be quite dry."—*Cobbett's E. Gram.*, ¶ 31.

OBS. 20.—When a compound, ending with any of the foregoing irregular words, is made plural, it follows the fashion of the word with which it ends: as, *Gentleman, gentlemen; bondwoman, bondwomen; foster-child, foster-children; solan-goose, solan-geese; eyetooth, eyeteeth; woodlouse, woodlice;*[143] *dormouse, dormice; half-penny, halfpence, half-pennies.* In this way, these irregularities extend to many words; though some of the metaphorical class, as *kite's-foot, colts-foot, bear's-foot, lion's-foot*, being names of plants, have no plural. The word *man*, which is used the most frequently in this way, makes more than seventy such compounds. But there are some words of this ending, which, not being compounds of *man*, are regular: as, *German, Germans; Turcoman, Turcomans;*

Mussulman, Mussulmans; talisman, talismans; leman, lemans; caiman, caimans.

OBS. 21.—Compounds, in general, admit but one variation to form the plural, and that must be made in the principal word, rather than in the adjunct; but where the terms differ little in importance, the genius of the language obviously inclines to a variation of the last only. Thus we write *fathers-in-law, sons-in-law, knights-errant, courts-martial, cousins-german, hangers-on, comings-in, goings-out, goings-forth,* varying the first; and *manhaters, manstealers, manslayers, maneaters, mandrills, handfuls, spoonfuls, mouthfuls, pailfuls, outpourings, ingatherings, downsittings, overflowings,* varying the last. So, in many instances, when there is a less intimate connexion of the parts, and the words are written with a hyphen, if not separately, we choose to vary the latter or last: as, *fellow-servants, queen-consorts, three-per-cents, he-goats, she-bears, jack-a-dandies, jack-a-lanterns, piano-fortes.* The following mode of writing is irregular in two respects; first, because the words are separated, and secondly, because both are varied: "Is it unreasonable to say with John Wesley, that '*men buyers* are exactly on a level with *men stealers*?"—GOODELL'S LECT. II: *Liberator,* ix, 65. According to analogy, it ought to be: "*Manbuyers* are exactly on a level with *manstealers.*" J. W. Wright alleges, that, "The phrase, 'I want two *spoonfuls* or *handfuls,*' though common, is improperly constructed;" and that, "we should say, 'Two *spoons* or *hands full.*'"—*Philos. Gram.,* p. 222. From this opinion, I dissent: both authority and analogy favour the former mode of expressing the plural of such quantities.

OBS. 22.—There is neither difficulty nor uncertainty respecting the proper forms for the plurals of compound nouns in general; but the two irregular words *man* and *woman* are often varied at the beginning of the looser kind of compounds, contrary to what appears to be the general analogy of similar words. Of the propriety of this, the reader may judge, when I shall have quoted a few examples: "Besides their *man-servants* and their *maid-servants*."—*Nehemiah*, vii, 67. "And I have oxen and asses, flocks, and *men-servants*, and *women-servants*."—*Gen.*, xxxii, 5. "I gat me *men-singers*, and *women-singers*, and the delights of the sons of men."—*Ecclesiastes*, ii, 8. "And she brought forth a *man-child*, who was to rule all nations with a rod of iron."—*Rev.*, xii, 5.—"Why have ye done this, and saved the *men-children* alive?"—*Exod.*, i, 18. Such terms as these, if thought objectionable, may easily be avoided, by substituting for the former part of the compound the separate adjective *male* or *female*; as, *male child*, *male children*. Or, for those of the third example, one might say, "*singing men* and *singing women*," as in *Nehemiah*, vii, 67; for, in the ancient languages, the words are the same. Alger compounds "*singing-men* and *singing-women*."

OBS. 23.—Some foreign compound terms, consisting of what are usually, in the language from which they come, distinct words and different parts of speech, are made plural in English, by the addition of *e* or *es* at the end. But, in all such cases, I think the hyphen should be inserted in the compound, though it is the practice of many to omit it. Of this odd sort of words, I quote the following examples from Churchill; taking the liberty to insert the hyphen, which he omits: "*Ave-Maries, Te-Deums, camera-obscuras, agnus-castuses, habeas-corpuses, scire-faciases, hiccius-docciuses, hocus-pocuses, ignis-fatuuses, chef-d'oeuvres, congé-d'élires, flower-de-luces, louis-d'-ores, tête-à-têtes.*"—*Churchill's Gram.*, p. 62.

OBS. 24.—Some nouns, from the nature of the things meant, have no plural. For, as there ought to be no word, or inflection of a word, for which we cannot conceive an appropriate meaning or use, it follows that whatever is of such a species that it cannot be taken in any plural sense, must naturally be named by a word which is singular only: as, *perry, cider, coffee, flax, hemp, fennel, tallow, pitch, gold, sloth, pride, meekness, eloquence.* But there are some things, which have in fact neither a comprehensible unity, nor any distinguishable plurality, and which may therefore be spoken of in either number; for the distinction of unity and plurality is, in such instances, merely verbal; and, whichever number we take, the word will be apt to want the other: as, *dregs,* or *sediment; riches,* or *wealth; pains,* or *toil; ethics,* or *moral philosophy; politics,* or *the science of government; belles-lettres,* or *polite literature.* So *darkness,* which in English appears to have no plural, is expressed in Latin by *tenebræ,* in French by *ténèbres,* which have no singular. It is necessary that every noun should be understood to be of one number or the other; for, in connecting it with a verb, or in supplying its place by a pronoun, we must assume it to be either singular or plural. And it is desirable that singulars and plurals should always abide by their appropriate forms, so that they may be thereby distinguished with readiness. But custom, which regulates this, as every thing else of the like nature, does not always adjust it well; or, at least, not always upon principles uniform in themselves and obvious to every intellect.

OBS. 25.—Nouns of multitude, when taken collectively, generally admit the regular plural form; which of course is understood with reference to the individuality of the whole collection, considered as one thing: but, when taken distributively, they have a plural signification without the form; and, in this case, their plurality refers to the individuals that compose the assemblage. Thus, a *council,* a *committee,* a *jury,* a *meeting,* a *society,* a *flock,* or a *herd,* is singular; and the regular plurals are *councils, committees, juries, meetings, societies, flocks, herds.* But these, and many similar words, may be taken plurally without the *s,* because a collective noun is the name of many individuals together. Hence we may say, "The *council were* unanimous."—"The *committee are* in consultation."—"The *jury were* unable to agree."—"The *meeting have shown their* discretion."—"The *society have settled their* dispute."—"The *flock are* widely scattered."—"The whole *herd were drowned* in the sea." The propriety of the last example seems questionable; because *whole* implies unity, and *were drowned* is plural. Where a purer concord can be effected, it may be well to avoid such a construction, though examples like it are not uncommon: as, "Clodius was acquitted by *a corrupt jury*, that had palpably taken shares of money before *they gave their* verdict."—*Bacon*. "And the *whole multitude* of the people *were praying* without, at the time of incense."—*Luke*, i, 10.

OBS. 26.—Nouns have, in some instances, a unity or plurality of meaning, which seems to be directly at variance with their form. Thus, *cattle*, for beasts of pasture, and *pulse*, for peas and beans, though in appearance singulars only, are generally, if not always, plural; and *summons, gallows, chintz, series, superficies, molasses, suds, hunks, jakes, trapes*, and *corps*, with the appearance of plurals, are generally, if not always, singular. Dr. Webster says that *cattle* is of both numbers; but wherein the oneness of cattle can consist, I know not. The Bible says, "God made—*cattle after their kind*."—*Gen.*, i, 25. Here *kind* is indeed singular, as if *cattle* were a natural genus of which one must be *a cattle*; as *sheep* are a natural genus of which one is *a sheep*: but whether properly expressed so or not, is questionable; perhaps it ought to be, "and cattle after their *kinds*." Dr. Gillies says, in his History of Greece, "*cattle was regarded* as the most convenient *measure* of value." This seems to me to be more inaccurate and unintelligible, than to say, "*Sheep was regarded* as the most convenient *measure* of value." And what would this mean? *Sheep* is not singular, unless limited to that number by some definitive word; and *cattle* I conceive to be incapable of any such limitation.

OBS. 27.—Of the last class of words above cited, some may assume an additional *es*, when taken plurally; as, *summonses, gallowses, chintses*: the rest either want the plural, or have it seldom and without change of form. *Corps*, a body of troops, is a French word, which, when singular, is pronounced *c=ore*, and when plural, *c=ores*. But *corpse*, a dead body, is an English word, pronounced *k~orps*, and making the plural in two syllables, *corpses*. *Summonses* is given in Cobb's Dictionary as the plural of *summons*; but some authors have used the latter with a plural verb: as, "But Love's first *summons* seldom *are* obey'd."—*Waller's Poems*, p. 8. Dr. Johnson says this noun is from the verb *to summon*; and, if this is its origin, the singular ought to be *a summon*, and then *summons* would be a regular plural. But this "singular noun with a plural termination," as Webster describes it, more probably originated from the Latin verb *submoneas*, used in the writ, and came to us through the jargon of law, in which we sometimes hear men talk of "*summonsing* witnesses." The authorities for it, however, are good enough; as, "*This* present *summons*."—SHAK.: *Joh. Dict.* "*This summons* he resolved to disobey."—FELL: *ib. Chints* is called by Cobb a "substantive *plural*" and defined as "cotton *cloths*, made in India;" but other lexicographers define it as singular, and Worcester (perhaps more properly) writes it *chintz*. Johnson cites Pope as speaking of "*a charming chints*," and I have somewhere seen the plural formed by adding es. "Of the Construction of single Words, or *Serieses* of Words."— *Ward's Gram.*, p. 114. Walker, in his Elements of Elocution, makes frequent use of the word "*serieses*," and of the phrase "*series of serieses*." But most writers, I suppose, would doubt the propriety of this practice; because, in Latin, all nouns of the fifth declension, such as *caries, congeries, series, species, superficies*, make their nominative and vocative cases alike in both numbers. This, however, is no rule for writing English. Dr. Blair has used the word *species* in a plural sense; though I think he ought rather to have preferred the regular English word *kinds*: "The higher *species* of poetry seldom *admit* it."—*Rhet.*, p. 403. *Specie*, meaning hard money, though derived or corrupted from *species*, is not the singular of that word; nor has it any occasion for a plural form, because we never speak of *a specie*. The plural of *gallows*, according to Dr. Webster, is *gallowses*; nor is that form without other authority, though some say, *gallows* is of both numbers and not to be varied: "*Gallowses* were occasionally put in order by the side of my windows."—*Leigh Hunt's Byron*, p. 369.

"Who would not guess there might be hopes,
The fear of *gallowses* and ropes,
Before their eyes, might reconcile
Their animosities a while?"—*Hudibras*, p. 90.

OBS. 28.—Though the plural number is generally derived from the singular, and of course must as generally imply its existence, we have examples, and those not a few, in which the case is otherwise. Some nouns, because they signify such things as nature or art has made plural or double; some, because they have been formed from other parts of speech by means of the plural ending which belongs to nouns; and some, because they are compounds in which a plural word is principal, and put last, are commonly used in the plural number only, and have, in strict propriety, no singular. Though these three classes of plurals may not be perfectly separable, I shall endeavour to exhibit them in the order of this explanation.

1. Plurals in meaning and form: *analects, annals,[144] archives, ashes, assets, billiards, bowels, breeches, calends, cates, chops, clothes, compasses, crants, eaves, embers, estovers, forceps, giblets, goggles, greaves, hards* or *hurds, hemorrhoids, ides, matins, nippers, nones, obsequies, orgies,[145] piles, pincers* or *pinchers, pliers, reins, scissors, shears, skittles, snuffers, spectacles, teens, tongs, trowsers, tweezers, umbles, vespers, victuals.*

2. Plurals by formation, derived chiefly from adjectives: *acoustics, aeronautics, analytics, bitters, catoptrics, commons, conics, credentials, delicates, dioptrics, economics, ethics, extraordinaries, filings, fives, freshes, glanders, gnomonics, goods, hermeneutics, hustings,*

hydrodynamics, hydrostatics, hydraulics, hysterics, inwards, leavings, magnetics, mathematics, measles, mechanics, mnemonics, merils, metaphysics, middlings, movables, mumps, nuptials, optics, phonics, phonetics, physics,[146] pneumatics, poetics, politics, riches, rickets, settlings, shatters, skimmings, spherics, staggers, statics, statistics, stays, strangles, sundries, sweepings, tactics, thanks, tidings, trappings, vives, vitals, wages,[147] withers, yellows.

3. Plurals by composition: *backstairs, cocklestairs, firearms,[148] headquarters, hotcockles, spatterdashes, self-affairs.* To these may be added the Latin words, *aborigines, antipodes, antes, antoeci, amphiscii, anthropophagi, antiscii, ascii, literati, fauces, regalia,* and *credenda,* with the Italian *vermicelli,* and the French *belles-lettres* and *entremets.*

OBS. 29.—There are several nouns which are set down by some writers as wanting the singular, and by others as having it. Of this class are the following: *amends,[149] ancients, awns, bots, catacombs, chives, cloves, cresses, dogsears, downs, dregs,[150] entrails, fetters, fireworks, greens, gyves, hatches, intestines, lees,[151] lungs, malanders, mallows, moderns, oats, orts, pleiads, premises, relics, remains, shackles, shambles,[152] stilts, stairs, tares, vetches.* The fact is, that these words have, or ought to have, the singular, as often as there is any occasion to use it; and the same may, in general terms, be said of other nouns, respecting the formation of *the plural.* [153] For where the idea of unity or plurality comes clearly before the mind, we are very apt to shape the word accordingly, without thinking much about the authorities we can quote for it.

OBS. 30.—In general, where both numbers exist in common use, there is some palpable oneness or individuality, to which the article *a* or *an* is applicable; the nature of the species is found entire in every individual of it; and a multiplication of the individuals gives rise to plurality in the name.

But the nature of a mass, or of an indefinite multitude taken collectively, is not found in individuals as such; nor is the name, whether singular, as *gold*, or plural, as *ashes*, so understood. Hence, though every noun must be of one number or the other, there are many which have little or no need of both. Thus we commonly speak of *wheat, barley, or oats*, collectively; and very seldom find occasion for any other forms of these words. But chafferers at the corn-market, in spite of Cobbett,[154] will talk about *wheats* and *barleys*, meaning different kinds[155] or qualities; and a gardener, if he pleases, will tell of an *oat*, (as does Milton, in his Lycidas,) meaning a single seed or plant. But, because *wheat* or *barley* generally means that sort of grain in mass, if he will mention a single kernel, he must call it a *grain of wheat* or a *barleycorn*. And these he may readily make plural, to specify any particular number; as, *five grains of wheat*, or *three barleycorns*.

OBS. 31.—My chief concern is with general principles, but the illustration of these requires many particular examples—even far more than I have room to quote. The word *amends* is represented by Murray and others, as being singular as well as plural; but Webster's late dictionaries exhibit *amend* as singular, and *amends* as plural, with definitions that needlessly differ, though not much. I judge "*an amends*" to be bad English; and prefer the regular singular, *an amend*. The word is of French origin, and is sometimes written in English with a needless final *e*; as, "But only to make a kind of honourable *amende* to God."—*Rollin's Ancient Hist.*, Vol. ii, p. 24. The word *remains* Dr. Webster puts down as plural only, and yet uses it himself in the singular: "The creation of a Dictator, even for a few months, would have buried every *remain* of freedom."—*Webster's Essays*, p. 70. There are also other authorities for this usage, and also for some other nouns that are commonly thought to have no singular; as, "But Duelling is unlawful and murderous, a *remain* of the ancient Gothic barbarity."—*Brown's Divinity*, p. 26. "I grieve with the old, for so many additional inconveniences, more than their small *remain* of life seemed destined to undergo."—POPE: *in Joh. Dict.* "A disjunctive syllogism is one whose major *premise* is disjunctive."—*Hedge's Logic.* "Where should he have this gold? It is some poor fragment, some slender *ort* of his remainder."—SHAK.: *Timon of Athens.*

OBS. 32.—There are several nouns which are usually alike in both numbers. Thus, *deer, folk, fry, gentry, grouse, hose, neat, sheep, swine, vermin,* and *rest,* (i. e. *the rest,* the others, the residue,) are regular singulars, but they are used also as plurals, and that more frequently. Again, *alms, aloes, bellows, means, news, odds, shambles,* and *species,* are proper plurals, but most of them are oftener construed as singulars. *Folk* and *fry* are collective nouns. *Folk* means *people*; *a folk, a people*: as, "The ants are *a people* not strong;"—"The conies are but *a feeble folk.*"—*Prov.,* xxx, 25, 26. "He laid his hands on a few sick *folk,* and healed *them.*"—*Mark,* vi, 5. *Folks,* which ought to be the plural of *folk,* and equivalent to *peoples,* is now used with reference to a plurality of individuals, and the collective word seems liable to be entirely superseded by it. A *fry* is a swarm of young fishes, or of any other little creatures living in water: so called, perhaps, because their motions often make the surface *fry.* Several such swarms might properly be called *fries*; but this form can never be applied to the individuals, without interfering with the other. "So numerous *was the fry.*"—*Cowper.* "The *fry betake themselves* to the neighbouring pools."—*Quarterly Review.* "You cannot think more contemptuously of *these gentry* than *they* were thought of by the true prophets."—*Watson's Apology,* p. 93. "*Grouse,* a heathcock."—*Johnson.*

"The 'squires in scorn will fly the house
For better game, and look for *grouse.*"—*Swift.*

"Here's an English tailor, come hither for stealing out of *a* French *hose.*"—*Shak.* "He, being in love, could not see to garter his *hose.*"—*Id.*

Formerly, the plural was *hosen*: "Then these men were bound, in their coats, their *hosen*, and their hats."—*Dan.*, iii, 21. Of *sheep*, Shakspeare has used the regular plural: "Two hot *sheeps*, marry!"—*Love's Labour Lost*, Act ii, Sc. 1.

"Who both by his calf and his lamb will be known,
May well kill *a neat* and *a sheep* of his own."—*Tusser.*

"His droves of asses, camels, herds of *neat*,
And flocks of *sheep*, grew shortly twice as great."—*Sandys.*

"As a jewel of gold in *a swine's* snout."—*Prov.*, xi, 22. "A herd of *many swine*, feeding."—*Matt.*, viii, 30. "An idle person only lives to spend his time, and eat the fruits of the earth, like a *vermin* or a wolf."—*Taylor.* "The head of a wolf, dried and hanged up, will scare away *vermin.*"—*Bacon.* "Cheslip, *a small vermin* that lies under stones or tiles."—SKINNER: in *Joh. and in Web. Dict.* "This is flour, the *rest is* bran."—"And the *rest were* blinded."—*Rom.*, xi, 7. "The poor beggar hath a just demand of *an alms.*"—*Swift.* "Thine *alms are* come up for a memorial before God."—*Acts*, x, 4. "The draught of air performed the function of *a bellows.*"—*Robertson's Amer.*, ii, 223. "As the *bellows do.*"—*Bicknell's Gram.*, ii, 11. "The *bellows are* burned."—*Jer.*, vi, 29. "Let *a gallows* be made."—*Esther*, v, 14. "*Mallows are* very useful in medicine."—*Wood's Dict.* "*News*," says Johnson, "is without the singular, unless it be considered as singular."—*Dict.* "So *is* good *news* from a far country."—*Prov.*, xxv, 25. "Evil *news rides* fast, while good *news baits.*"—*Milton.* "When Rhea heard *these news*, she fled."—*Raleigh.* "*News were brought* to the queen."—*Hume's Hist.*, iv, 426. "The *news* I bring *are* afflicting, but the consolation with which *they* are attended, ought to moderate your grief."—*Gil Blas*, Vol. ii, p. 20. "Between these two cases there *are* great *odds.*"—*Hooker.* "Where the *odds is* considerable."—*Campbell.* "Determining on which side the *odds lie.*"—

Locke. "The greater *are the odds* that he mistakes his author."—*Johnson's Gram. Com.*, p. 1. "Though thus *an odds* unequally they meet."—*Rowe's Lucan*, B. iv, l. 789. "Preëminent by so *much odds*."—*Milton.* "To make a *shambles* of the parliament house."—*Shak.* "The earth has been, from the beginning, a great Aceldama, *a shambles* of blood."—*Christian's Vade-Mecum*, p. 6. "*A shambles*" sounds so inconsistent, I should rather say, "*A shamble.*" Johnson says, the etymology of the word is *uncertain*; Webster refers it to the Saxon *scamel*: it means *a butcher's stall, a meat-market*; and there would seem to be no good reason for the *s*, unless more than one such place is intended. "Who sells his subjects to the *shambles* of a foreign power."—*Pitt.* "A special idea is called by the schools *a species.*"—*Watts.* "He intendeth the care of *species*, or common natures."—*Brown.* "ALOE, (al~o) *n.; plu.* ALOES."—*Webster's Dict.*, and *Worcester's.* "But it was *aloe* itself to lose the reward."— *Tupper's Crock of Gold*, p. 16.

"But high in amphitheatre above,
His arms the everlasting *aloes* threw."
—*Campbell*, G. of W., ii, 10.

OBS. 33.—There are some nouns, which, though really regular in respect to possessing the two forms for the two numbers, are not free from irregularity in the manner of their application. Thus *means* is the regular plural of *mean*; and, when the word is put for mediocrity, middle point, place, or degree, it takes both forms, each in its proper sense; but when it signifies things instrumental, or that which is used to effect an object, most writers use *means* for the singular as well as for the plural:[156] as, "By *this means*"—"By *those means*," with reference to one mediating cause; and, "By *these means*,"—"By *those means*," with reference to more than one. Dr. Johnson says the use of *means* for *mean* is not very grammatical; and, among his examples for the true use of the word, he has the following: "Pamela's noble heart would needs gratefully make known the valiant *mean* of her safety."—*Sidney.* "Their virtuous conversation was a *mean* to work the heathens' conversion."—*Hooker.* "Whether his wits should by that *mean* have been taken from him."—*Id.* "I'll devise a *mean* to draw the Moor out of the way."—*Shak.* "No place will please me so, no *mean* of death."—*Id.* "Nature is made better by no *mean*, but nature makes that *mean*."—*Id.* Dr. Lowth also questioned the propriety of construing *means* as singular, and referred to these same authors as authorities for preferring the regular form. Buchanan insists that *means* is right in the plural only; and that, "The singular should be used as perfectly analogous; by this *mean*, by that *mean*."—*English Syntax,* p. 103. Lord Kames, likewise, appears by his practice to have been of the same opinion: "Of this the child must be sensible intuitively, for it has no other *mean* of knowledge."—*Elements of Criticism,* Vol. i, p. 357. "And in both the same *mean* is employed."—*Ib.* ii, 271. Caleb Alexander, too, declares "*this means,*" "*that means.*" and "*a means,*" to be "ungrammatical."—*Gram.,* p. 58. But common usage has gone against the suggestions of these critics, and later grammarians have rather confirmed the irregularity, than attempted to reform it.

OBS. 34.—Murray quotes sixteen good authorities to prove that means may be singular; but whether it *ought* to be so or not, is still a disputable point. Principle is for the regular word *mean,* and good practice favours the irregularity, but is still divided. Cobbett, to the disgrace of grammar, says, "*Mean,* as a noun, is *never used in the singular.* It, like some other words, has broken loose from all principle and rule. By universal consent, it *is become always a plural,* whether used with *singular or plural* pronouns and articles, *or not.*"—*E. Gram.,* p. 144. This is as ungrammatical, as it is untrue. Both mean and means are sufficiently authorized in the singular: "The prospect which by this mean is opened to you."—*Melmoth's Cicero.* "Faith in this doctrine never terminates in itself, but is *a mean,* to holiness as an end."—*Dr. Chalmers, Sermons,* p. v. "The *mean* of basely affronting him."—*Brown's Divinity,* p. 19. "They used every *mean* to prevent the reestablishment of their religion."—*Dr Jamieson's Sacred Hist.*, i, p. 20. "As a necessary *mean* to prepare men for the discharge of that duty."—*Bolingbroke, on Hist.*, p. 153. "Greatest is the power of a *mean*, when its power is least suspected."—*Tupper's Book of Thoughts*, p. 37. "To the deliberative orator the reputation of unsullied virtue is not only useful, as a *mean* of promoting his general influence, it is also among his most efficient engines of persuasion, upon every individual occasion."—*J. Q. Adams's Lectures on Rhetoric and Oratory*, i, 352. "I would urge it upon you, as the most effectual *mean* of extending your respectability and usefulness in the world."—*Ib.*, ii, 395. "Exercise will be admitted to be a necessary *mean* of improvement."—*Blair's Rhet.*, p. 343. "And by *that means* we have now an early prepossession in their favour."—*Ib.*, p. 348. "To abolish all sacrifice by revealing a better *mean* of reconciliation." —*Keith's Evidences*, p. 46. "As a *mean* of destroying the distinction." —*Ib.*, p. 3. "Which however is by no *mean* universally the case."— *Religious World Displayed*, Vol. iii, p. 155.

OBS. 35.—Again, there are some nouns, which, though they do not lack the regular plural form, are sometimes used in a plural sense without the plural termination. Thus *manner* makes the plural *manners*, which last is now generally used in the peculiar sense of behaviour, or deportment, but not always: it sometimes means methods, modes, or ways; as, "At sundry times and in divers *manners*."—*Heb.*, i, 1. "In the *manners* above mentioned."—*Butler's Analogy*, p. 100. "There be three *manners* of trials in England."—COWELL: *Joh. Dict., w. Jury*. "These two *manners* of representation."—*Lowth's Gram.*, p. 15. "These are the three primary modes, or *manners*, of expression."—*Lowth's Gram.*, p. 83. "In arrangement, too, various *manners* suit various styles."—*Campbell's Phil. of Rhet.*, p. 172. "Between the two *manners*."—*Bolingbroke, on Hist.*, p. 35. "Here are three different *manners* of asserting."— *Barnard's Gram.*, p. 59. But *manner* has often been put for *sorts*, without the *s*; as, "The tree of life, which bare *twelve manner* of fruits."—*Rev.*, xxii, 2. "All *manner* of men assembled here in arms."—*Shak.* "All *manner* of outward advantages."—*Atterbury.* Milton used *kind* in the same way, but not very properly; as, "All *kind* of living creatures."—*P. Lost*, B. iv, l. 286. This irregularity it would be well to avoid. *Manners* may still, perhaps, be proper for modes or ways; and *all manner*, if allowed, must be taken in the sense of a collective noun; but for sorts, kinds, classes, or species, I would use neither the plural nor the singular of this word. The word *heathen*, too, makes the regular plural *heathens*, and yet is often used in a plural sense without the *s*; as, "Why do the *heathen* rage?"—*Psalms*, ii, 1. "Christianity was formerly propagated among the *heathens*."—*Murray's Key*, 8vo, p. 217. The word *youth*, likewise, has the same peculiarities.

OBS. 36.—Under the present head come names of fishes, birds, or other things, when the application of the singular is extended from the individual to the species, so as to supersede the plural by assuming its construction: as, Sing. "A great *fish*."—*Jonah*, i, 17. Plur. "For the multitude of *fishes*'."—*John*, xxi, 6. "A very great multitude of *fish*."—*Ezekiel*, xlvii, 9.[157] The name of the genus being liable to this last construction, men seem to have thought that the species should follow; consequently, the regular plurals of some very common names of fishes are scarcely known at all. Hence some grammarians affirm, that *salmon, mackerel, herring, perch, tench*, and several others, are alike in both numbers, and ought never to be used in the plural form. I am not so fond of honouring these anomalies. Usage is here as unsettled, as it is arbitrary; and, if the expression of plurality is to be limited to either form exclusively, the regular plural ought certainly to be preferred. But, *for fish taken in bulk*, the singular form seems more appropriate; as, "These vessels take from thirty-eight to forty-five quintals of *cod* and *pollock*, and six thousand barrels of *mackerel*, yearly."—*Balbi's Geog.*, p. 28.

OBS. 37.—The following examples will illustrate the unsettled usage just mentioned, and from them the reader may judge for himself what is right. In quoting, at second-hand, I generally think it proper to make double references; and especially in citing authorities after Johnson, because he so often gives the same passages variously. But he himself is reckoned good authority in things literary. Be it so. I regret the many proofs of his fallibility. "Hear you this Triton of the *minnows?*"—*Shak.* "The shoal of *herrings* was of an immense extent."—*Murray's Key*, p. 185. "Buy my *herring* fresh."—SWIFT: *in Joh. Dict.* "In the fisheries of Maine, *cod, herring, mackerel alewives, salmon,* and other *fish,* are taken."—*Balbi's Geog.*, p. 23. "MEASE, *n.* The quantity of 500; as, a *mease* of *herrings.*"—*Webster's Dict.* "We shall have plenty of *mackerel* this season."—ADDISON: *in Joh. Dict.* "*Mackarel* is the same in both numbers. Gay has improperly *mackarels.*"—*Churchill's Gram.*, p. 208. "They take *salmon* and *trouts* by groping and tickling them under the bellies."—CAREW: *in Joh. Dict.* "The pond will keep *trout* and *salmon* in their seasonable plight."—*Id., ib., w. Trout.* "Some *fish* are preserved fresh in vinegar, as *turbot.*"—*Id., ib., w. Turbot.* "Some *fish* are boiled and preserved fresh in vinegar, as *tunny* and *turbot.*"—*Id., ib., w. Tunny.* "Of round *fish,* there are *brit, sprat, barn, smelts.*"—*Id., ib., w. Smelt.* "For *sprats* and *spurlings* for your house."—TUSSEE: *ib., w. Spurling.* "The coast is plentifully stored with *pilchards, herrings,* and *haddock.*"—CAREW: *ib., w. Haddock.* "The coast is plentifully stored with round *fish, pilchard, herring, mackerel,* and *cod*"—*Id., ib., w. Herring.* "The coast is plentifully stored with *shellfish, sea-hedgehogs, scallops, pilcherd, herring,* and *pollock.*"—*Id., ib., w. Pollock.* "A *roach* is *a fish* of no great reputation for his dainty taste. It is noted that *roaches* recover strength and grow a fortnight after spawning."—WALTON: *ib., w. Roach.* "A friend of mine stored a pond of three or four acres with *carps* and *tench.*"—HALE: *ib., w. Carp.* "Having stored a very great pond with *carps, tench,* and other *pond-fish,* and only put in two small *pikes,* this pair of tyrants in seven years devoured the whole."—*Id., ib., w. Tench.* "Singular, *tench*; plural, *tenches.*"—*Brightland's Gram.*, p. 78. "The polar bear preys upon *seals, fish*, and the carcasses of *whales.*"—*Balbi's Geog.*, p. 172. "*Trouts* and *salmons* swim against the stream."—BACON: *Ward's Gram.*, p. 130.

"'Tis true no *turbots* dignify my boards,
But *gudgeons, flounders*, what my Thames affords."—*Pope.*

OBS. 38.—Prom the foregoing examples it would seem, if fish or fishes are often spoken of without a regular distinction of the grammatical numbers, it is not because the words are not susceptible of the inflection, but because there is some difference of meaning between the mere name of the sort and the distinct modification in regard to number. There are also other nouns in which a like difference may be observed. Some names of building materials, as *brick, stone, plank, joist*, though not destitute of regular plurals, as *bricks, stones, planks, joists*, and not unadapted to ideas distinctly singular, as *a brick, a stone, a plank, a joist*, are nevertheless sometimes used in a plural sense without the *s*, and sometimes in a sense which seems hardly to embrace the idea of either number; as, "Let us make *brick*, and burn *them* thoroughly."—*Gen.*, xi, 3. "And they had *brick* for *stone.*"—*Ib.* "The tale of *bricks.*"—*Exod.*, v, 8 and 18. "Make *brick.*"—*Ib.*, v, 16. "From your *bricks.*"—*Ib.*, v, 19. "Upon altars of *brick.*"—*Isaiah.* lxv, 3. "The *bricks* are fallen down."—*Ib.*, ix, 10. The same variety of usage occurs in respect to a few other words, and sometimes perhaps without good reason; as, "Vast numbers of sea *fowl* frequent the rocky cliffs."—*Balbi's Geog.*, p. 231. "Bullocks, sheep, and *fowls.*"—*Ib.*, p. 439. "*Cannon* is used alike in both numbers."—*Everest's Gram.*, p. 48. "*Cannon* and *shot* may be used in the singular or plural sense."—*O. B. Peirce's Gram.*, p. 37. "The column in the Place Vendome is one hundred and thirty-four feet high, and is made of the brass of the *cannons* taken from the Austrians and

Prussians."—*Balbi's Geog.*, p. 249. "As his *cannons* roar."—*Dryden's Poems*, p. 81. "Twenty *shot* of his greatest cannon."—CLARENDON: *Joh. Dict.* "Twenty *shots*" would here, I think, be more proper, though the word is not made plural when it means *little balls of lead.* "And *cannons* conquer armies."—*Hudibras*, Part III, Canto iii, l. 249.

"Healths to both kings, attended with the roar
Of *cannons* echoed from th' affrighted shore."—*Waller*, p. 7.

OBS. 39.—Of foreign nouns, many retain their original plural; a few are defective; and some are redundant, because the English form is also in use. Our writers have laid many languages under contribution, and thus furnished an abundance of irregular words, necessary to be explained, but never to be acknowledged as English till they conform to our own rules.

1. Of nouns in *a, saliva*, spittle, and *scoria*, dross, have no occasion for the plural; *lamina*, a thin plate, makes *laminæ*; *macula*, a spot, *maculæ*; *minutia*, a little thing, *minutiæ*; *nebula*, a mist, *nebulæ*; *siliqua*, a pod, *siliqiuæ*. *Dogma* makes *dogmas* or *dogmata*; *exanthema*, *exanthemas* or *exanthemata*; *miasm* or *miasma*, *miasms* or *miasmata*; *stigma*, *stigmas* or *stigmata*.

2. Of nouns in *um*, some have no need of the plural; as, *bdellium, decorum, elysium, equilibrium, guaiacum, laudanum, odium, opium, petroleum, serum, viaticum*. Some form it regularly; as, *asylums, compendiums, craniums, emporiums, encomiums, forums, frustums, lustrums, mausoleums, museums, pendulums, nostrums, rostrums, residuums, vacuums*. Others take either the English or the Latin plural; as, *desideratums* or *desiderata, mediums* or *media, menstruums* or *menstrua, memorandums* or *memoranda, spectrums* or *spectra, speculums* or *specula, stratums* or *strata, succedaneums* or *succedanea, trapeziums* or *trapezia, vinculums* or *vincula*. A few seem to have the Latin plural only: as,

arcanum, arcana; datum, data; effluvium, effluvia; erratum, errata; scholium, scholia.

3. Of nouns in *us*, a few have no plural; as, *asparagus, calamus, mucus.* Some have only the Latin plural, which usually changes *us* to *i*; as, *alumnus, alumni; androgynus, androgyni; calculus, calculi; dracunculus, dracunculi; echinus, echini; magus, magi.* But such as have properly become English words, may form the plural regularly in *es*; as, *chorus, choruses:* so, *apparatus, bolus, callus, circus, fetus, focus, fucus, fungus, hiatus, ignoramus, impetus, incubus, isthmus, nautilus, nucleus, prospectus, rebus, sinus, surplus.* Five of these make the Latin plural like the singular; but the mere English scholar has no occasion to be told which they are. *Radius* makes the plural *radii* or *radiuses. Genius* has *genii*, for imaginary spirits, and *geniuses*, for men of wit. *Genus*, a sort, becomes *genera* in Latin, and *genuses* in English. *Denarius* makes, in the plural, *denarii* or *denariuses.*

4. Of nouns in *is*, some are regular; as, *trellis, trellises:* so, *annolis, butteris, caddis, dervis, iris, marquis, metropolis, portcullis, proboscis.* Some seem to have no need of the plural; as, *ambergris, aqua-fortis, arthritis, brewis, crasis, elephantiasis, genesis, orris, siriasis, tennis.* But most nouns of this ending follow the Greek or Latin form, which simply changes *is* to *=es*: as, *amanuensis, amanuenses; analysis, analyses; antithesis, antitheses; axis, axes; basis, bases; crisis, crises; diæresis, diæreses; diesis, dieses; ellipsis, ellipses; emphasis, emphases; fascis, fasces; hypothesis, hypotheses; metamorphosis, metamorphoses; oasis, oases; parenthesis, parentheses; phasis, phases; praxis, praxes; synopsis, synopses; synthesis, syntheses; syrtis, syrtes; thesis, theses.* In some, however, the original plural is not so formed; but is made by changing *is* to ~*ides*; as, *aphis, aphides; apsis, apsides; ascaris, ascarides; bolis, bolides; cantharis, cantharides; chrysalis, chrysalides; ephemeris, ephemerides;*

epidermis, epidermides. So *iris* and *proboscis*, which we make regular; and perhaps some of the foregoing may be made so too. Fisher writes *Praxises* for *praxes*, though not very properly. See his *Gram,* p. v. *Eques*, a Roman knight, makes *equites* in the plural.

5. Of nouns in *x*, there are few, if any, which ought not to form the plural regularly, when used as English words; though the Latins changed *x* to *ces*, and *ex* to *ices*, making the *i* sometimes long and sometimes short: as, *apex, apices*, for *apexes; appendix, appendices*, for *appendixes; calix, calices*, for *calixes; calx, calces*, for *calxes; calyx, calyces*, for *calyxes; caudex, caudices*, for *caudexes; cicatrix, cicatrices*, for *cicatrixes; helix, helices*, for *helixes; index, indices*, for *indexes; matrix, matrices*, for *matrixes; quincunx, quincunces*, for *quincunxes; radix, radices*, for *radixes; varix, varices*, for *varixes; vertex, vertices*, for *vertexes; vortex, vortices*, for *vortexes*. Some Greek words in *x* change that letter to *ges*; as, *larynx, larynges*, for *larinxes; phalanx, phalanges*, for *phalanxes*. *Billet-doux*, from the French, is *billets-doux* in the plural.

6. Of nouns in *on*, derived from Greek, the greater part always form the plural regularly; as, *etymons, gnomons, ichneumons, myrmidons, phlegmons, trigons, tetragons, pentagons, hexagons, heptagons, octagons, enneagons, decagons, hendecagons, dodecagons, polygons*. So *trihedrons, tetrahedrons, pentahedrons*, &c., though some say, these last may end in *dra*, which I think improper. For a few words of this class, however, there are double plurals in use; as, *automata* or *atomatons, criteria* or *criterions, parhelia* or *parhelions*; and the plural of *phenomenon* appears to be always *phenomena*.

7. The plural of *legumen* is *legumens* or *legumina*; of *stamen, stamens* or *stamina*: of *cherub, cherubs* or *cherubim*; of *seraph, seraphs* or *seraphim*; of *beau, beaus* or *beaux*; of *bandit, bandits* or *banditti*. The regular forms

are in general preferable. The Hebrew plurals *cherubim* and *seraphim*, being sometimes mistaken for singulars, other plurals have been formed from them; as, "And over it the *cherubims* of glory."—*Heb.* ix, 5. "Then flow one of the *seraphims* unto me."—*Isaiah*, vi, 6. Dr. Campbell remarks: "We are authorized, both by use and by analogy, to say either *cherubs* and *seraphs*, according to the English idiom, or *cherubim* and *seraphim*, according to the oriental. The former suits better the familiar, the latter the solemn style. I shall add to this remark," says he, "that, as the words *cherubim* and *seraphim* are plural, the terms *cherubims* and *seraphims*, as expressing the plural, are quite improper."—*Phil. of Rhet.*, p. 201.

OBS. 40.—When other parts of speech become nouns, they either want the plural, or form it regularly,[158] like common nouns of the same endings; as, "His affairs went on at *sixes* and *sevens*."—*Arbuthnot*. "Some mathematicians have proposed to compute by *twoes*; *others*, by *fours*; *others*, by *twelves*."—*Churchill's Gram.*, p. 81. "Three *fourths*, nine *tenths*."—*Ib.*, p. 230. "Time's *takings* and *leavings*."— *Barton*. "The *yeas* and *nays*."—*Newspaper*. "The *ays* and *noes*."—*Ib.* "Oes* and *spangles*."— *Bacon*. "The *ins* and the *outs*."—*Newspaper*."—We find it more safe against *outs* and *doubles*."—*Printer's Gram.* "His *ands* and his *ors*."—*Mott*. "One of the *buts*."—*Fowle*. "In raising the mirth of *stupids*."—*Steele*. "*Eatings, drinkings, wakings, sleepings, walkings, talkings, sayings, doings* —all were for the good of the public; there was not such a things as a secret in the town."—LANDON: *Keepsake*, 1833. "Her innocent *forsooths* and *yesses*."—*Spect.*, No. 266.

"Henceforth my wooing mind shall be expressed
In russet *yeas* and honest kersey *noes*."
—SHAK. See *Johnson's Dict., w. Kersey.*

GENDERS.

Genders, in grammar, are modifications that distinguish objects in regard to sex.

There are three genders; the *masculine*, the *feminine*, and the *neuter*.

The *masculine gender* is that which denotes persons or animals of the male kind; as, *man, father, king.*

The *feminine gender* is that which denotes persons or animals of the female kind; as, *woman, mother, queen.*

The *neuter gender* is that which denotes things that are neither male nor female; as, *pen, ink, paper.*

Hence, names of males are masculine; names of females, feminine; and names of things inanimate, literally, neuter.

Masculine nouns make regular feminines, when their termination is changed to *ess*: as, *hunter, huntress*; *prince, princess*; *lion, lioness.*

OBSERVATIONS.

OBS. 1.—The different genders in grammar are founded on the natural distinction of sex in animals, and on the absence of sex in other things. In English, they belong only to nouns and pronouns; and to these they are usually applied, not arbitrarily, as in some other languages, but agreeably to the order of nature. From this we derive a very striking advantage over those who use the gender differently, or without such rule; which is, that our pronouns are easy of application, and have a fine effect when objects are personified. Pronouns are of the same gender as the nouns for which they stand.

OBS. 2.—Many nouns are equally applicable to both sexes; as, *cousin, friend, neighbour, parent, person, servant.* The gender of these is usually determined by the context; and they are to be called masculine or feminine accordingly. To such words, some grammarians have applied the unnecessary and improper term *common gender.* Murray justly observes, "There is no such gender belonging to the language. The business of parsing can be effectually performed, without having recourse to a *common gender.*"—*Gram.,* 8vo. p. 39. The term is more useful, and less liable to objection, as applied to the learned languages; but with us, whose genders *distinguish objects in regard to sex,* it is plainly a solecism.

OBS. 3.—A great many of our grammars define gender to be "*the distinction of sex,*" and then speak of a *common gender,* in which the two sexes are left *undistinguished*; and of the *neuter gender,* in which objects are treated as being of *neither sex.* These views of the matter are obviously inconsistent. Not genders, or a gender, do the writers undertake to define, but "gender" as a whole; and absurdly enough, too; because this whole of gender they immediately distribute into certain *other genders,* into genders of gender, or kinds of gender, and these not compatible with their definition. Thus Wells: "Gender is *the distinction* of objects, with regard to sex. There are four genders;—the *masculine,* the *feminine,* the *common,* and the *neuter.*"—*School Gram.,* 1st Ed., p. 49. [Those] "Nouns which are applicable *alike to both sexes,* are of the *common* gender."—*Ib.* This then is manifestly no gender under the foregoing definition, and the term *neuter* is made somewhat less appropriate by the adoption of a third denomination before it. Nor is there less absurdity in the phraseology with which Murray proposes to avoid the recognition of the *common gender*: "Thus we may say, *Parents* is a noun of the *masculine and feminine* gender; *Parent,* if doubtful, is of the *masculine or feminine* gender; and *Parent,* if the gender is known by the construction, is of the gender so ascertained."—*Gram.,* 8vo, p. 39. According to this, we must have *five genders,* exclusive of that which is called *common*; namely, the *masculine*, the *feminine*, the *neuter*, the *androgynal*, and the *doubtful*.

OBS. 4.—It is plain that many writers on grammar have had but a confused notion of what a gender really is. Some of them, confounding gender with sex, deny that there are more than two genders, because there are only two sexes. Others, under a like mistake, resort occasionally, (as in the foregoing instance,) to an *androgynal*, and also to a *doubtful* gender: both of which are more objectionable than the *common gender* of the old grammarians; though this *common* "distinction with regard to sex," is, in our language, confessedly, no distinction at all. I assume, that there are in English the three genders, masculine, feminine, and neuter, and no more; and that every noun and every pronoun must needs be of some gender; consequently, of some one of these three. A gender is, literally, a sort, a kind, a sex. But genders, *in grammar*, are attributes of words, rather than of persons, or animals, or things; whereas sexes are attributes, not of words, but of living creatures. He who understands this, will perceive that the absence of sex in some things, is as good a basis for a grammatical distinction, as the presence or the difference of it in others; nor can it be denied, that the neuter, according to my definition, is a gender, is a distinction "in *regard* to sex," though it does not embrace either of the sexes. There are therefore three genders, and only three.

OBS. 5.—Generic names, even when construed as masculine or feminine, often virtually include both sexes; as, "Hast thou given *the horse* strength? hast thou clothed *his* neck with thunder? Canst thou make *him* afraid as a grasshopper? the glory of *his* nostrils is terrible."—*Job*, xxxix, 19. "Doth *the hawk* fly by thy wisdom, and stretch *her* wings toward the south? Doth *the eagle* mount up at thy command, and make *her* nest on high?"—*Ib.*, ver. 26. These were called, by the old grammarians, *epicene* nouns—that is, *supercommon*; but they are to be parsed each according to the gender of the pronoun which is put for it.

OBS. 6.—The gender of words, in many instances, is to be determined by the following principle of universal grammar. Those terms which are equally applicable to both sexes, (if they are not expressly applied to females,) and those plurals which are known to include both sexes, should be called masculine in parsing; for, in all languages, the masculine gender is considered the most worthy,[159] and is generally employed when both sexes are included under one common term. Thus *parents* is always masculine, and must be represented by a masculine pronoun, for the gender of a word is a property indivisible, and that which refers to the male sex, always takes the lead in such cases. If one say, "Joseph took *the young child and his mother* by night, and fled with *them* into Egypt," the pronoun *them* will be masculine; but let "*his*" be changed to *its*, and the plural pronoun that follows, will be feminine. For the feminine gender takes precedence of the neuter, but not of the masculine; and it is not improper to speak of a young child without designating the sex. As for such singulars as *parent, friend, neighbour, thief, slave*, and many others, they are feminine when expressly applied to any of the female sex; but otherwise, masculine.

OBS. 7.—Nouns of multitude, when they convey the idea of unity or take the plural form, are of the neuter gender; but when they convey the idea of plurality without the form, they follow the gender of the individuals which compose the assemblage. Thus a *congress*, a *council*, a *committee*, a *jury*, a *sort*, or a *sex*, if taken collectively, is neuter; being represented in discourse by the neuter pronoun *it*: and the formal plurals, *congresses, councils, committees, juries, sorts, sexes*, of course, are neuter also. But, if I say, "The committee disgraced *themselves*," the noun and pronoun are presumed to be masculine, unless it be known that I am speaking of a committee of females. Again: "The *fair sex, whose* task is not to mingle in the labours of public life, have *their* own part assigned *them* to act."—*Comly's Gram.*, p. 132. Here *sex*, and the three pronouns which have that word for their antecedent, are all feminine. Again: "*Each sex*, dressing *themselves* in the clothes of the other."—*Wood's Dictionary*, v. *Feast of Purim*. Here *sex*, and the pronoun which follows, are masculine; because, the male sex, as well as the female, is here spoken of plurally.

OBS. 8.—To *persons*, of every description, known or unknown, real or imaginary, we uniformly ascribe sex.[160] But, as personality implies intelligence, and sex supposes some obvious difference, a *young child* may be spoken of with distinction of sex or without, according to the notion of the speaker; as, "I went to see the *child* whilst they were putting on *its* cloaths.".—*Priestley's Gram.*, p. 125. "Because the *child* has no idea of any nurse besides *his* own."—*Ib.*, p. 153. To *brute animals* also, the same distinction is generally applied, though with less uniformity. Some that are very small, have a gender which seems to be merely occasional and figurative; as, "Go to the *ant*, thou sluggard; consider *her* ways, and be wise."—*Prov.*, vi, 6. "The *spider* taketh hold with *her* hands, and is in kings' palaces."—*Prov.*, xxx, 28. So the *bee* is usually made feminine, being a little creature of admirable industry and economy. But, in general, irrational creatures whose sex is unknown, or unnecessary to be regarded, are spoken of as neuter; as, "And it became a *serpent*; and Moses fled from before *it*. And the Lord said unto Moses, Put forth thine hand, and take *it* by the tail. And he put forth his hand and caught *it*, and *it* became a rod in his hand."—*Exod.*, iv, 3, 4. Here, although the word *serpent* is sometimes masculine, the neuter pronoun seems to be more proper. So of some imaginary creatures: as, "*Phenix*, the fowl which is said to exist single, and to rise again from *its* own ashes."—*Webster's Dict.* "So shall the *Phoenix* escape, with no stain on *its* plumage."—*Dr. Bartlett's Lect.*, p. 10.

OBS. 9.—But this liberty of representing animals as of no sex, is often carried to a very questionable extent; as, "The *hare* sleeps with *its* eyes open."—*Barbauld.* "The *hedgehog,* as soon as *it* perceives *itself* attacked, rolls *itself* into a kind of ball, and presents nothing but *its* prickles to the foe."—*Blair's Reader,* p. 138. "The *panther* is a ferocious creature: like the tiger *it* seizes *its* prey by surprise."—*Ib.,* p. 102. "The *leopard,* in *its* chace of prey, spares neither man nor beast."—*Ib.,* p. 103. "If a man shall steal an *ox,* or a *sheep,* and kill *it,* or sell *it.*"—*Exod.,* xxii, 1. "A *dog* resists *its* instinct to run after a hare, because *it* recollects the beating *it* has previously received on that account. The *horse* avoids the stone at which *it* once has stumbled."—*Spurzheim, on Education,* p. 3. "The *racehorse* is looked upon with pleasure; but it is the *warhorse,* that carries grandeur in *its* idea."—*Blair's Rhet.,* p. 30.

OBS. 10.—The sexes are distinguished *by words,* in four different ways. First, by the use of different terminations: as, *Jew, Jewess; Julius, Julia; hero, heroine.* Secondly, by the use of entirely different names: as, *Henry, Mary; king, queen.* Thirdly, by compounds or phrases including some distinctive term: as, *Mr. Murray, Mrs. Murray; Englishman, Englishwoman; grandfather, grandmother; landlord, landlady; merman, mermaid; servingman, servingmaid; man-servant, maid-servant; schoolmaster, schoolmistress; school-boy, school-girl; peacock, peahen; cock-sparrow, hen-sparrow; he-goat, she-goat; buck-rabbit, doe-rabbit; male elephant, female elephant; male convicts, female convicts.* Fourthly, by the pronouns *he, his, him,* put for nouns masculine; and *she, her, hers,* for nouns feminine: as, "Ask *him* that fleeth, and *her* that escapeth, and say, What is done?"—*Jer.,* xlviii, 19.

"O happy *peasant!* Oh unhappy *bard! His* the mere tinsel, *hers* the rich reward."—*Cowper.*

OBS. 11.—For feminine nouns formed by inflection, the regular termination is *ess*; but the manner in which this ending is applied to the original or masculine noun, is not uniform:—

1. In some instances the syllable *ess* is simply added: as, *accuser, accuseress; advocate, advocatess; archer, archeress; author, authoress; avenger, avengeress; barber, barberess; baron, baroness; canon, canoness; cit, cittess;[161] coheir, coheiress; count, countess; deacon, deaconess; demon, demoness; diviner, divineress; doctor, doctoress; giant, giantess; god, goddess; guardian, guardianess; Hebrew, Hebrewess; heir, heiress; herd, herdess; hermit, hermitess; host, hostess; Jesuit, Jesuitess; Jew, Jewess; mayor, mayoress; Moabite, Moabitess; monarch, monarchess; pape, papess*; or, *pope, popess; patron, patroness; peer, peeress; poet, poetess; priest, priestess; prior, prioress; prophet, prophetess; regent, regentess; saint, saintess; shepherd, shepherdess; soldier, soldieress; tailor, tailoress; viscount, viscountess; warrior, warrioress.*

2. In other instances, the termination is changed, and there is no increase of syllables: as, *abbot, abbess; actor, actress; adulator, adulatress; adulterer, adulteress; adventurer, adventuress; advoutrer, advoutress; ambassador, ambassadress; anchorite, anchoress*; or, *anachoret, anachoress; arbiter, arbitress; auditor, auditress; benefactor, benefactress; caterer, cateress; chanter, chantress; cloisterer, cloisteress; commander, commandress; conductor, conductress; creator, creatress; demander, demandress; detractor, detractress; eagle, eagless; editor, editress; elector, electress; emperor, emperess*, or *empress; emulator, emulatress; enchanter, enchantress; exactor, exactress; fautor, fautress; fornicator, fornicatress; fosterer, fosteress*, or *fostress; founder, foundress; governor, governess; huckster, huckstress*; or, *hucksterer, hucksteress; idolater, idolatress; inhabiter, inhabitress; instructor, instructress; inventor, inventress; launderer, launderess*, or *laundress; minister, ministress; monitor,*

monitress; murderer, murderess; negro, negress; offender, offendress; ogre, ogress; porter, portress; progenitor, progenitress; protector, protectress; proprietor, proprietress; pythonist, pythoness; seamster, seamstress; solicitor, solicitress; songster, songstress; sorcerer, sorceress; suitor, suitress; tiger, tigress; traitor, traitress; victor, victress; votary, votaress.

3. In a few instances the feminine is formed as in Latin, by changing *or* to *rix*; but some of these have also the regular form, which ought to be preferred: as, *adjutor, adjutrix; administrator, administratrix; arbitrator, arbitratrix; coadjutor, coadjutrix; competitor, competitress,* or *competitrix; creditor, creditrix; director, directress,* or *directrix; executor, executress,* or *executrix; inheritor, inheritress,* or *inheritrix; mediator, mediatress,* or *mediatrix; orator, oratress,* or *oratrix; rector, rectress,* or *rectrix; spectator, spectatress,* or *spectatrix; testator, testatrix; tutor, tutoress,* or *tutress,* or *tutrix; deserter, desertress,* or *desertrice,* or *desertrix.*

4. The following are irregular words, in which the distinction of sex is chiefly made by the termination: *amoroso, amorosa: archduke, archduchess; chamberlain, chambermaid; duke, duchess; gaffer, gammer; goodman, goody; hero, heroine; landgrave, landgravine; margrave, margravine; marquis, marchioness; palsgrave, palsgravine; sakeret, sakerhawk; sewer, sewster; sultan, sultana; tzar, tzarina; tyrant, tyranness; widower, widow.*

OBS. 12.—The proper names of persons almost always designate their sex; for it has been found convenient to make the names of women different from those of men. We have also some appellatives which correspond to each other, distinguishing the sexes by their distinct application to each: as, *bachelor, maid; beau, belle; boy, girl; bridegroom, bride; brother, sister; buck, doe; boar, sow; bull, cow; cock, hen; colt, filly; dog, bitch; drake, duck; earl, countess; father, mother; friar, nun; gander, goose; grandsire, grandam; hart, roe; horse, mare; husband, wife; king, queen; lad, lass; lord, lady; male, female; man, woman; master, mistress*; Mister, Missis; (Mr., Mrs.;) *milter, spawner; monk, nun; nephew, niece; papa, mamma; rake, jilt; ram, ewe; ruff, reeve; sire, dam; sir, madam; sloven, slut; son, daughter; stag, hind; steer, heifer; swain, nymph; uncle, aunt; wizard, witch; youth, damsel; young man, maiden.*

OBS. 13.—The people of a particular country are commonly distinguished by some name derived from that of their country; as, *Americans, Africans, Egyptians, Russians, Turks.* Such words are sometimes called *gentile names.* There are also adjectives, of the same origin, if not the same form, which correspond with them. "Gentile names are for the most part considered as masculine, and the feminine is denoted by the gentile adjective and the noun *woman*: as, a *Spaniard*, a *Spanish woman*; a *Pole*, or *Polander*, a *Polish woman*. But, in a few instances, we always use a compound of the adjective with *man* or *woman*: as, an *Englishman*, an *Englishwoman*; a *Welshman*, a *Welshwoman*; an *Irishman*, an *Irishwoman*; a *Frenchman*, a *Frenchwoman*; a *Dutchman*, a *Dutchwoman*: and in these cases the adjective is employed as the collective noun; as, *the Dutch, the French,* &c. A *Scotchman*, and a *Scot*, are both in use; but the latter is not common in prose writers: though some employ it, and these generally adopt the plural, *Scots*, with the definite article, as the collective term."—*Churchill's New Gram.*, p. 70.

OBS. 14.—The names of things without life, used literally, are always of the neuter gender: as, "When Cleopatra fled, Antony pursued her in a five-oared galley; and, coming along side of her *ship*, entered *it* without being seen by her."—*Goldsmith's Rome*, p. 160. "The *sun*, high as *it* is, has *its* business assigned; and so have the stars."—*Collier's Antoninus*, p. 138. But inanimate objects are often represented figuratively as having sex. Things remarkable for power, greatness, or sublimity, are spoken of as masculine;

as, the *sun, time, death, sleep, fear, anger, winter, war*. Things beautiful, amiable, or prolific, are spoken of as feminine; as, a *ship*, the *moon*, the *earth, nature, fortune, knowledge, hope, spring, peace*. Figurative gender is indicated only by the personal pronouns of the singular number: as, "When we say of the *sun, He* is setting; or of a *ship, She* sails well."—*L. Murray*. For these two objects, the *sun* and a *ship*, this phraseology is so common, that the literal construction quoted above is rarely met with.

OBS. 15.—When any inanimate object or abstract quality is distinctly personified, and presented to the imagination in the character of a living and intelligent being, there is necessarily a change of the gender of the word; for, whenever personality is thus ascribed to what is literally neuter, there must be an assumption of one or the other sex: as, "*The Genius of Liberty* is awakened, and springs up; *she* sheds her divine light and creative powers upon the two hemispheres. A great *nation*, astonished at seeing *herself* free, stretches *her* arms from one extremity of the earth to the other, and embraces the first nation that became so."—*Abbé Fauchet*. But there is an inferior kind of personification, or of what is called such, in which, so far as appears, the gender remains neuter: as, "The following is an instance of personification and apostrophe united: 'O *thou sword* of the Lord! how long will it be ere *thou* be quiet? put *thyself* up into *thy* scabbard, rest, and be still! How can *it* be quiet, seeing the Lord hath given *it* a charge against Askelon, and against the sea-shore? there hath he appointed *it*.'"—*Murray's Gram.*, p. 348. See *Jer.*, xlvii, 6.

OBS. 16.—If what is called personification, does not always imply a change of gender and an ascription of sex, neither does a mere ascription of sex to what is literally of no sex, necessarily imply a personification; for there may be sex without personality, as we see in brute animals. Hence the gender of a brute animal personified in a fable, may be taken literally as before; and the gender which is figuratively ascribed to the *sun*, the *moon*, or a *ship*, is merely metaphorical. In the following sentence, *nature* is animated and made feminine by a metaphor, while a lifeless object bearing the name of *Venus*, is spoken of as neuter: "Like that conceit of old, which declared that the *Venus of Gnidos* was not the work of Praxiteles, since *nature herself* had concreted the boundary surface of *its* beauty."—*Rush, on the Voice*, p. xxv.

OBS. 17.—"In personifications regard must be had to propriety in determining the gender. Of most of the passions and moral qualities of man the ancients formed deities, as they did of various other things: and, when these are personified, they are usually made male or female, according as they were gods or goddesses in the pagan mythology. The same rule applies in other cases: and thus the planet Jupiter will be masculine; Venus, feminine: the ocean, *Oce=anus*, masculine: rivers, months, and winds, the same: the names of places, countries, and islands, feminine."—*Churchill's Gram.*, p. 71.

OBS. 18.—These suggestions are worthy of consideration, but, for the gender which ought to be adopted in personifications, there seems to be no absolute general rule, or none which English writers have observed with much uniformity. It is well, however, to consider what is most common in each particular case, and abide by it. In the following examples, the sex ascribed is not that under which these several objects are commonly figured; for which reason, the sentences are perhaps erroneous:—

"*Knowledge* is proud that *he* has learn'd so much; *Wisdom* is humble that *he* knows no more."—*Cowper*.

"But hoary *Winter*, unadorned and bare,
Dwells in the dire retreat, and freezes there;
There *she* assembles all her blackest storms,
And the rude hail in rattling tempests forms."—*Addison*.

"*Her* pow'r extends o'er all things that have breath,
A cruel tyrant, and *her* name is *Death*."—*Sheffield*.

CASES.

Cases, in grammar, are modifications that distinguish the relations of nouns or pronouns to other words.

There are three cases; the *nominative,* the *possessive,* and the *objective.*

The *nominative case* is that form or state of a noun or pronoun, which usually denotes the subject of a finite verb: as, The *boy* runs; *I* run.

The subject of a finite verb is that which answers to *who* or *what* before it; as, "The boy runs."—*Who* runs? "The *boy.*" Boy is therefore here in the *nominative* case.

The *possessive case* is that form or state of a noun or pronoun, which usually denotes the relation of property: as, The *boy's* hat; *my* hat.

The possessive case of nouns is formed, in the singular number, by adding to the nominative *s preceded by an apostrophe*; and, in the plural, when the nominative ends in *s*, by adding *an apostrophe only*: as, singular, *boy's*; plural, *boys'*;—sounded alike, but written differently.

The *objective case* is that form or state of a noun or pronoun which usually denotes the object of a verb, participle, or preposition: as, I know the *boy,* having seen *him* at *school*; and he knows *me.*

The object of a verb, participle, or preposition, is that which answers to *whom* or *what* after it; as, "I know the boy."—I know *whom*? "The boy."

Boy is therefore here in the *objective* case.

The nominative and the objective of nouns, are always alike in form, being distinguishable from each other only by their place in a sentence, or by their simple dependence according to the sense.

OBSERVATIONS.

OBS. 1.—The cases, in grammar, are founded on the different relations under which things are represented in discourse; and from which the words acquire correspondent relations; or connexions and dependences according to the sense. In Latin, there are six cases; and in Greek, five. Consequently, the nouns and pronouns of those languages, and also their adjectives and participles, (which last are still farther inflected by the three genders,) are varied by many different terminations unknown to our tongue. In English, those modifications or relations which we call cases, belong only to nouns and pronouns; nor are there ever more than three. Pronouns are not necessarily like their antecedents in case.

OBS. 2.—Because the infinitive mood, a phrase, or a sentence, may in some instances be made the subject of a verb, so as to stand in that relation in which the nominative case is most commonly found; very many of our grammarians have deliberately represented all terms used in this manner, as being "*in the nominative case*:" as if, to sustain any one of the relations which are usually distinguished by a particular case, must necessarily constitute that modification itself. Many also will have participles, infinitives, phrases, and sentences, to be occasionally "*in the objective case*:" whereas it must be plain to every reader, that they are, all of them, *indeclinable* terms; and that, if used in any relation common to nouns or pronouns, they assume that office, as participles, as infinitives, as phrases, or as sentences, and not as *cases*. They no more take the nature of cases, than they become nouns or pronouns. Yet Nixon, by assuming that *of*, with the word governed by it, constitutes a *possessive case*, contrives to give to participles, and even to the infinitive mood, *all three of the cases*. Of the infinitive, he says, "An examination of the first and second methods of parsing this mood, must naturally lead to the inference that *it is a substantive*; and that, if it has the nominative case, it must also have the possessive and objective cases of a substantive. The fourth method proves its [capacity of] being in the possessive case: thus, 'A desire *to learn*;' that is, '*of learning.*' When it follows a participle, or a verb, as by the fifth or [the] seventh method, it is in the objective case. Method sixth is analogous to the Case Absolute of a substantive."—*Nixon's Parser*, p. 83. If the infinitive mood is really a *declinable substantive*, none of our grammarians have placed it in the right chapter; except that bold contemner of all grammatical and literary authority, Oliver B. Peirce. When will the cause of learning cease to have assailants and underminers among those who profess to serve it? Thus every new grammatist, has some grand absurdity or other, peculiar to himself; and what can be more gross, than to talk of English infinitives and participles as being in the *possessive case*?

OBS. 3.—It was long a subject of dispute among the grammarians, what number of cases an English noun should be supposed to have. Some, taking the Latin language for their model, and turning certain phrases into cases to fill up the deficits, were for having *six* in each number; namely, the nominative, the genitive, the dative, the accusative, the vocative, and the ablative. Others, contending that a case in grammar could be nothing else than a terminational inflection, and observing that English nouns have but one case that differs from the nominative in form, denied that there were more than two, the nominative and the possessive. This was certainly an important question, touching a fundamental principle of our grammar; and any erroneous opinion concerning it, might well go far to condemn the book that avouched it. Every intelligent teacher must see this. For what sense could be made of parsing, without supposing an objective case to nouns? or what propriety could there be in making the words, *of,* and *to,* and *from,* govern or compose three different cases? Again, with what truth can it be said, that nouns have *no cases* in English? or what reason can be assigned for making more than three?

OBS. 4.—Public opinion is now clear in the decision, that it is *expedient* to assign to English nouns three cases, and no more; and, in a matter of this kind, what is expedient for the purpose of instruction, is right. Yet, from the works of our grammarians, may be quoted every conceivable notion, right or wrong, upon this point. Cardell, with Tooke and Gilchrist on his side, contends that English nouns have *no cases.* Brightland averred that they have neither cases nor genders.[162] Buchanan, and the author of the old British Grammar, assigned to them *one* case only, the possessive, or genitive. Dr. Adam also says, "In English, nouns have *only one case,* namely, the genitive, or possessive case."—*Latin and Eng. Gram.,* p. 7. W. B. Fowle has two cases, but rejects the word *case*: "We use the simple term *agent* for a *noun that acts,* and *object* for the object of an action."—*Fowle's True Eng. Gram.,* Part II, p. 68. Spencer too discards the word *case,* preferring "*form,*" that he may merge in one the nominative and the objective, giving to nouns *two* cases, but neither of these. "Nouns have *two Forms,* called the *Simple* and [the] *Possessive.*"—*Spencer's E. Gram.,* p. 30. Webber's Grammar, published at Cambridge in 1832, recognizes but *two* cases of nouns, declaring the objective to be "altogether superfluous."—P. 22. "Our substantives have no more cases than two."—*Jamieson's Rhet.,* p. 14. "A Substantive doth not properly admit of more than two cases: the Nominative, and the Genitive."—*Ellen Devis's Gram.,* p. 19. Dr. Webster, in his Philosophical Grammar, of 1807, and in his Improved Grammar, of 1831, teaches the same doctrine, but less positively. This assumption has also had the support of Lowth, Johnson, Priestley, Ash, Bicknell, Fisher, Dalton, and our celebrated Lindley Murray.[163] In Child's or Latham's

English Grammar, 1852, it is said, "The cases in the present English are three:—1. Nominative; 2. Objective; 3. Possessive." But this seems to be meant of pronouns only; for the next section affirms, "The *substantives* in English *have only two* out of the three cases."—See pp. 79 and 80. Reckless of the current usage of grammarians, and even of self-consistency, both author and reviser will have no objective case of nouns, because this is like the nominative; yet, finding an objective set after "the adjective *like*," they will recognize it as "*a dative* still existing in English!"—See p. 156. Thus do they forsake their own enumeration of cases, as they had before, in all their declensions, forsaken the new order in which they had at first so carefully set them!

OBS. 5.—For the *true* doctrine of *three* cases, we have the authority of Murray, in his later editions; of Webster, in his "Plain and Comp. Grammar, grounded on *True Principles*," 1790; also in his "Rudiments of English Grammar," 1811; together with the united authority of Adams, Ainsworth, Alden, Alger, Bacon, Barnard, Bingham, Burr, Bullions, Butler, Churchill, Chandler, Cobbett, Cobbin, Comly, Cooper, Crombie, Davenport, Davis, Fisk,
A. Flint, Frost, Guy, Hart, Hiley, Hull, Ingersoll, Jaudon, Kirkham,
Lennie, Mack, M'Culloch, Maunder, Merchant, Nixon, Nutting, John Peirce,
Perley, Picket, Russell, Smart, R. C. Smith, Rev. T. Smith, Wilcox, and I know not how many others.

OBS. 6.—Dearborn, in 1795, recognized *four* cases: "the nominative, the possessive, the objective, and the absolute."—*Columbian Gram.*, pp. 16 and 20. Charles Bucke, in his work misnamed "A Classical Grammar of the English Language," published in London in 1829, asserts, that, "Substantives in English do not vary their terminations;" yet he gives them *four* cases; "the nominative, the genitive, the accusative, and the vocative."

So did Allen, in a grammar much more classical, dated, London, 1813. Hazen, in 1842, adopted "four cases; namely, the nominative, the possessive, the objective, and the independent."—*Hazen's Practical Gram.*, p. 35. Mulligan, since, has chosen these four: "Nominative, Genitive, Dative, Accusative."—*Structure of E. Lang.*, p. 185. And yet his case after *to* or *for* is *not* "*dative*," but "*accusative!*"— *Ib.*, p. 239. So too, Goodenow, of Maine, makes the cases four: "the *subjective*,[164] the *possessive*, the *objective*, and the *absolute*."—*Text-Book*, p. 31. Goldsbury, of Cambridge, has also four: "the Nominative, the Possessive, the Objective, and the Vocative."—*Com. S. Gram.*, p. 13. Three other recent grammarians,— Wells, of Andover,— Weld, of Portland,—and Clark, of Bloomfield, N. Y., —also adopt "*four* cases;—the *nominative*, the *possessive*, the *objective*, and the *independent*."—*Wells's Gram.*, p. 57; *Weld's*, 60; *Clark's*, 49. The first of these gentlemen argues, that, "Since a noun or pronoun, used *independently*, cannot at the same time be employed as 'the subject of a verb,' there is a manifest impropriety in regarding it as a *nominative*." It might as well be urged, that a nominative after a verb, or in apposition with an other, is, for this reason, not a *nominative*. He also cites this argument: "'Is there not as much difference between the *nominative* and [the] *independent* case, as there is between the *nominative* and [the] *objective?* If so, why class them together as *one* case?'—*S. R. Hall*."—*Wells's School Gram.*, p. 51. To this I answer, No. "The nominative is that case which *primely denotes the name* of any person or thing;" (*Burn's Gram.*, p. 36;) and *this only* it is, that can be absolute, or independent, in English. This scheme of four cases is, in fact, a grave innovation. As authority for it, Wells cites Felton; and bids his readers, "See also Kennion, Parkhurst, Fowle, Flint, Goodenow, Buck, Hazen, Goldsbury, Chapin, S. Alexander, and P. Smith."—Page 57. But is the fourth case of these authors *the same* as his? Is it a case which "has usually the nominative form," but admits occasionally of "*me*" and "*him*," and embraces objective nouns of "*time*, *measure, distance, direction,* or *place*?" No. Certainly one half of them, and probably more, give little or no countenance to *such* an independent case as he has adopted. Parkhurst admitted but three cases; though he thought *two others* "might be an improvement." What Fowle has said in support of Wells's four cases, I have sought with diligence, and not found. Felton's "independent case" is only what he absurdly calls, "*The noun or pronoun addressed.*"— Page 91. Bucke and Goldsbury acknowledge "*the nominative case absolute*;" and none of the twelve, so far as I know, admit any objective word, or what others call objective, to be independent or absolute, except perhaps Goldsbury.

OBS. 7.—S. R. Hall, formerly principal of the Seminary for Teachers at Andover, (but no great grammarian,) in 1832, published a manual, called "The Grammatical Assistant;" in which he says, "There are *at least five cases,* belonging to English nouns, differing as much from *each* other, as the cases of Latin and Greek nouns. They may be called Nominative, Possessive, Objective, Independent and Absolute."—P. 7. O. B. Peirce will have both nouns and pronouns to be used in *five cases,* which he thus enumerates: "Four simple cases; the Subjective, Possessive, Objective, and the Independent; and the Twofold case."—*Gram.,* p. 42. But, on page 56th, he speaks of a "twofold *subjective* case," "the twofold *objective* case," and shows how the *possessive* may be twofold also; so that, without taking any of the Latin cases, or even all of Hall's, he really recognizes as many as seven, if not eight. Among the English grammars which assume all the *six cases* of the Latin Language, are Burn's, Coar's, Dilworth's, Mackintosh's, Mennye's, Wm. Ward's, and the "Comprehensive Grammar," a respectable little book, published by Dobson of Philadelphia, in 1789, but written by somebody in England.

OBS. 8.—Of the English grammars which can properly be said to be *now in use,* a very great majority agree in ascribing to nouns three cases, and three only. This, I am persuaded, is the best number, and susceptible of the best defence, whether we appeal to authority, or to other argument. The disputes of grammarians make no small part of the *history of grammar*; and in submitting to be guided by their decisions, it is proper for us to consider what *degree of certainty* there is in the rule, and what difference or concurrence there is among them: for, the teaching of any other than the best opinions, is not the teaching of science, come from what quarter it may. On the question respecting the objective case of nouns, Murray and Webster *changed sides with each other*; and that, long after they first appeared as grammarians. Nor was this the only, or the most important instance, in which the different editions of the works of these two gentlemen, present them in opposition, both to themselves and to each other. "What cases are there in English? The *nominative*, which usually stands before a verb; as, the *boy* writes: The *possessive*, which takes an *s* with a *comma*, and denotes property; as, *John's* hat: The *objective*, which follows a verb or preposition; as, he honors *virtue*, or it is an honor to *him*."—*Webster's Plain and Comp. Gram., Sixth Edition*, 1800, p. 9. "But for convenience, the two positions of nouns, one *before*, the other *after* the verb, are called *cases*. There are then three cases, the *nominative, possessive*, and *objective*."—*Webster's Rudiments of Gram.*, 1811, p. 12. "In English therefore names have two cases only, the *nominative* or simple name, and the *possessive*."— *Webster's Philosoph. Gram.*, 1807, p. 32: also his *Improved Gram.*, 1831, p. 24.

OBS. 9.—Murray altered his opinion after the tenth or eleventh edition of his duodecimo Grammar. His instructions stand thus: "In English, substantives have but two cases, the nominative, and [the] possessive or genitive."—*Murray's Gram. 12mo, Second Edition*, 1796, p. 35. "For the assertion, that there are in English but two cases of nouns, and three of pronouns, we have the authority of Lowth, Johnson, Priestley, &c. *names which are sufficient* to decide this point."—*Ib.*, p. 36. "In English, substantives have three cases, the nominative, the possessive, and the objective."—*Murray's Gram.*, *12mo, Twenty-third Edition*, 1816, p. 44. "The author of this work *long doubted* the propriety of assigning to English substantives an *objective case*: but a renewed critical examination of the subject; an examination to which he was prompted by the extensive and increasing demand for the grammar, has produced in his mind *a full persuasion*, that the nouns of our language are entitled to this comprehensive objective case."—*Ib.*, p. 46. If there is any credit in changing one's opinions, it is, doubtless, in changing them for the better; but, of all authors, a grammarian has the most need critically to examine his subject before he goes to the printer. "This case was adopted in the *twelfth edition* of the Grammar."—*Murray's Exercises*, 12mo, N. Y., 1818, p. viii.

OBS. 10.—The *possessive case* has occasioned no less dispute than the objective. On this vexed article of our grammar, custom has now become much more uniform than it was a century ago; and public opinion may be said to have settled most of the questions which have been agitated about it. Some individuals, however, are still dissatisfied. In the first place, against those who have thought otherwise, it is determined, by infinite odds of authority, that there *is such a case*, both of nouns and of pronouns. Many a common reader will wonder, who can have been ignorant enough to deny it. "The learned and sagacious Wallis, to whom every English grammarian owes a tribute of reverence, calls this modification of the noun an *adjective possessive*; I think, with no more propriety than he might have applied the same to the Latin genitive."—*Dr. Johnson's Gram.*, p. 5. Brightland also, who gave to *adjectives* the name of *qualities*, included all possessives among them, calling them "*Possessive Qualities*, or *Qualities of Possession*."—*Brightland's Gram.*, p. 90.

OBS. 11.—This exploded error, William S. Cardell, a few years ago, republished as a novelty; for which, among other pretended improvements of a like sort, he received the ephemeral praise of some of our modern literati. William B. Fowle also teaches the same thing. See his *Common School Gram.*, Part II, p. 104. In Felch's Grammar, too, published in Boston in 1837, an attempt is made, to revive this old doctrine; but the author takes no notice of any of the above-named authorities, being probably ignorant of them all. His *reasoning* upon the point, does not appear to me to be worthy of a detailed answer.[165] That the possessive case of nouns is not an adjective, is demonstrable; because it may have adjectives of various kinds, relating to it: as, "*This old man's* daughter."—*Shak.* It may also govern an other possessive; as, "*Peter's wife's* mother."—*Bible.* Here the former possessive is governed by the latter; but, if both were adjectives, they would both relate to the noun *mother*, and so produce a confusion of ideas. Again, nouns of the possessive case have a distinction of number, which adjectives have not. In gender also, there lies a difference. Adjectives, whenever they are varied by gender or number, *agree with their nouns* in these respects. Not so with possessives; as, "In the *Jews'* religion."—*Gal.*, i. 13. "The *children's* bread."—*Mark*, vii, 27. "Some *men's* sins."—*1 Tim.*, v, 24. "Other *men's* sins."—*Ib.*, ver. 22.

OBS. 12.—Secondly, general custom has clearly determined that the possessive case of *nouns* is always to be written *with an apostrophe*: except in those few instances in which it is not governed singly by the noun following, but so connected with an other that both are governed jointly; as, "*Cato the Censor's* doctrine,"—"*Sir Walter Scott's* Works,"—"*Beaumont* and *Fletcher's Plays.*" This custom of using the apostrophe, however, has been opposed by many. Brightland, and Buchanan, and the author of the British Grammar, and some late writers in the Philological Museum, are among those who have successively taught, that the possessive case should be formed *like the nominative plural*, by adding *s* when the pronunciation admits the sound, and *es* when the word acquires an additional syllable. Some of these approve of the apostrophe, and others do not. Thus Brightland gives some examples, which are contrary to his rule, adopting that strange custom of putting the *s* in Roman, and the name in Italic; "as, King *Charles*'s *Court*, and St. *James*'s *Park*."—*Gram. of the English Tongue*, p. 91.

OBS. 13.—"The genitive case, in my opinion," says Dr. Ash, "might be much more properly formed by adding *s*, or when the pronunciation requires it, *es*, without an Apostrophe: as, *men, mens; Ox, Oxes; Horse, Horses; Ass, Asses*."—*Ash's Gram.*, p. 23. "To write *Ox's, Ass's, Fox's*, and at the same time pronounce it *Oxes, Asses, Foxes*, is such a departure from the original formation, at least in writing, and such an inconsistent use of the Apostrophe, as cannot be equalled perhaps in any other language."—*Ib.* Lowth, too, gives some countenance to this objection: "It [i.e., *'God's grace'*] was formerly written *'Godis grace;'* we now always shorten it with an apostrophe; often *very improperly*, when we are obliged to pronounce it fully; as, *'Thomas's* book,' that is, *'Thomasis* book,' not *'Thomas his* book,' as it is commonly supposed."—*Lowth's Gram.*, p. 17. Whatever weight there may be in this argument, the objection has been overruled by general custom. The convenience of distinguishing, even to the eye alone, the numbers and cases of the noun, is found too great to be relinquished. If the declension of English nouns is ever to be amended, it cannot be done in this way. It is understood by every reader, that the *apostrophic s* adds a syllable to the noun, whenever it will not unite with the sound in which the nominative ends; as, *torch's*, pronounced *torchiz*.

"Yet time ennobles or degrades each line;
It brightened *Craggs's*, and may darken thine."—*Pope.*

OBS. 14.—The English possessive case unquestionably originated in that form of the Saxon genitive which terminates in *es*, examples of which may be found in almost any specimen of the Saxon tongue: as, "On *Herodes* dagum,"—"In *Herod's* days;"—"Of *Aarones* dohtrum,"—"Of *Aaron's* daughters."—*Luke*, i, 5. This ending was sometimes the same as that of the plural; and both were changed to *is* or *ys*, before they became what we now find them. This termination added a syllable to the word; and Lowth suggests, in the quotation above, that the apostrophe was introduced to shorten it. But some contend, that the use of this mark originated in a mistake. It appears from the testimony of Brightland, Johnson, Lowth, Priestley, and others, who have noticed the error in order to correct it, that an opinion was long entertained, that the termination *'s* was a contraction of the word *his*. It is certain that Addison thought so; for he expressly says it, in the 135th number of the Spectator. Accordingly he wrote, in lieu of the regular possessive, "My paper is *Ulysses his* bow."—*Guardian*, No. 98. "Of *Socrates his* rules of prayer."—*Spect.*, No. 207. So Lowth quotes Pope: "By *young Telemachus his* blooming years."—*Lowth's Gram.*, p. 17.[166] There is also one late author who says, "The *'s* is a contraction of *his*, and was formerly written in full; as, William Russell *his* book."—*Goodenow's Gram.*, p. 32. This is undoubtedly bad English; and always was so, however common may have been the erroneous notion which gave rise to it. But the apostrophe, whatever may have been its origin, is now the acknowledged distinctive mark of the possessive case of English nouns. The application of the *'s*, frequently to feminines, and sometimes to plurals, is proof positive that it is *not a contraction* of the pronoun *his*; as,

"Now Jove suspends his golden scales in air,
Weighs the *men's* wits against the *Lady's* hair."
—*Pope*, R. of L., C. v, l. 72.

OBS. 15.—Many of the old grammarians, and Guy, Pinneo, and Spencer, among the moderns, represent the regular formation of the possessive case as being the same in both numbers, supposing generally in the plural an abbreviation of the word by the omission of the second or syllabic *s*. That is, they suppose that such terms as *eagles' wings, angels' visits*, were written for *eagles's wings, angels's visits*, &c. This odd view of the matter accounts well enough for the fashion of such plurals as *men's, women's, children's*, and makes them regular. But I find no evidence at all of the fact on which these authors presume; nor do I believe that the regular possessive plural was ever, in general, a syllable longer than the nominative. If it ever had been so, it would still be easy to prove the point, by citations from ancient books. The general principle then is, that *the apostrophe forms the possessive case, with an s in the singular, and without it in the plural*; but there are some exceptions to this rule, on either hand; and these must be duly noticed.

OBS. 16.—The chief exceptions, or irregularities, in the formation of the possessive *singular*, are, I think, to be accounted mere poetic licenses; and seldom, if ever, to be allowed in prose. Churchill, (closely copying Lowth,) speaks of them thus: "In poetry the *s* is frequently omitted after proper names ending in *s* or *x* as, 'The wrath of *Peleus'* son.' *Pope*. This is scarcely allowable in prose, though instances of it occur: as, '*Moses'* minister.' *Josh.*, i, 1. '*Phinehas'* wife.' *1 Sam.*, iv, 19. 'Festus came into *Felix'* room.' *Acts*, xxiv, 27. It was done in prose evidently to avoid the recurrence of a sibilant sound at the end of two following syllables; but this may as readily be obviated by using the preposition *of*, which is now commonly substituted for the possessive case in most instances."—*Churchill's New Gram.*, p. 215. In Scott's Bible, Philadelphia, 1814, the texts here quoted are all of them corrected, thus: "*Moses's* minister,"—"*Phinehas's* wife,"—"*Felix's* room." But the phrase, "for *conscience* sake," (*Rom.*, xiii, 5,) is there given without the apostrophe. Alger prints it, "for *conscience'* sake," which is better; and though not regular, it is a common form for this particular expression. Our common Bibles have this text: "And the weaned child shall put his hand on the *cockatrice'* den."—*Isaiah*, xi, 8. Alger, seeing this to be wrong, wrote it, "on the *cockatrice-den*."—*Pronouncing Bible*. Dr. Scott, in his Reference Bible, makes this possessive regular, "on the *cockatrice's* den." This is right.

The Vulgate has it, "*in caverna reguli;*" which, however, is not classic Latin. After *z* also, the poets sometimes drop the *s*: as,

"Sad was the hour, and luckless was the day,
When first from *Shiraz'* walls I bent my way."—*Collins.*

OBS. 17.—A recent critic, who, I think, has not yet learned to speak or write the possessive case of *his own name* properly, assumes that the foregoing occasional or poetical forms are the only true ones for the possessive singular of such words. He says, "When the name *does end* with the sound of *s* or *z*, (no matter what letter represents the sound,) the possessive form *is made* by annexing only an apostrophe."—*O. B. Peirce's Gram.*, p. 44. Agreeably to this rule, he letters his work, "*Peirce' Grammar,*" and condemns, as bad English, the following examples and all others like them: "James *Otis's* letters, General *Gates's* command, General *Knox's* appointment, Gov. *Meigs's* promptness, Mr. *Williams's* oration, The *witness's* deposition."—*Ib.*, p. 60. It is obvious that this gentleman's doctrine and criticism are as contrary to the common practice of all good authors, as they are to the common grammars, which he ridicules. Surely, such expressions as, "*Harris's* Hermes, *Philips's* Poems, *Prince's* Bay, *Prince's* Island, *Fox's* Journal, King *James's* edict, a *justice's* warrant, *Sphinx's* riddle, the *lynx's* beam, the *lass's* beauty," have authority enough to refute the cavil of this writer; who, being himself wrong, falsely charges the older grammarians, that," their theories vary from the principles of the language correctly spoken or written."—*Ib.*, p. 60. A much more judicious author treats this point of grammar as follows: "When the possessive noun is singular, and terminates with an *s*, another *s* is requisite after it, and the apostrophe must be placed between the two; as, '*Dickens's* works,'—'*Harris's* wit.'"—*Day's Punctuation, Third London Edition*, p. 136. The following example, too, is right: "I would not yield to be your *house's* guest."—*Shakespeare.*

OBS. 18.—All *plural* nouns that differ from the singular without ending in *s*, form the possessive case in the same manner as the singular: as, *man's, men's; woman's, women's j child's, children's; brother's, brothers' or brethren's; ox's, oxen's; goose, geese's.* In two or three words which are otherwise alike in both numbers, the apostrophe ought to follow the *s* in the plural, to distinguish it from the singular: as, the *sheep's* fleece, the *sheeps'* fleeces; a *neat's* tongue, *neats'* tongues; a *deer's* horns, a load of *deers'* horns.

OBS. 19.—Dr. Ash says, "Nouns of the plural number that end in *s*, will not very properly admit of the genitive case."—*Ash's Gram.,* p. 54. And Dr. Priestley appears to have been of the same opinion. See his *Gram.,* p. 69. Lowth too avers, that the sign of the possessive case is "never added to the plural number ending in *s*."—*Gram.,* p. 18. Perhaps he thought the plural sign must involve an other *s*, like the singular. This however is not true, neither is Dr. Ash's assertion true; for the New Testament speaks as properly of "the *soldiers'* counsel," as of the "*centurion's* servant;" of "the scribes that were of the *Pharisees'* part," as of "*Paul's sister's* son." It would appear, however, that the possessive plural is less frequently used than the possessive singular; its place being much oftener supplied by the preposition *of* and the objective. We cannot say that either of them is absolutely necessary to the language; but they are both worthy to be commended, as furnishing an agreeable variety of expression.

> "Then shall *man's* pride and dulness comprehend
> His *actions', passions', being's* use and end."—*Pope.*

OBS. 20.—The apostrophe was introduced into the possessive case, at least for the singular number, in some part of the seventeenth century. Its adoption for the plural, appears to have been later: it is not much used in books a hundred years old. In Buchanan's "Regular English Syntax," which was written, I know not exactly when, but near the middle of the eighteenth century, I find the following paragraph: "We have certainly a Genitive Plural, though there has been no Mark to distinguish it. The Warriors Arms, i. e. the Arms of the Warriors, is as much a Genitive Plural, as the Warrior's Arms, for the Arms of the Warrior is a Genitive Singular. To distinguish this Genitive Plural, especially to Foreigners, we might use the Apostrophe reversed, thus, the Warrior`s Arms, the Stone`s End, for the End of the Stones, the Grocer`s, Taylor`s, Haberdasher`s, &c. Company; for the Company of Grocers, Taylors, &c. The Surgeon`s Hall, for the Hall of the Surgeons; the Rider`s Names, for the Names of the Riders; and so of all Plural Possessives."—See *Buchan. Synt.*, p. 111. Our present form of the possessive plural, being unknown to this grammarian, must have had a later origin; nor can it have been, as some imagine it was, an abbreviation of a longer and more ancient form.

OBS. 21.—The apostrophic *s* has often been added to nouns *improperly*; the words formed by it not being intended for the possessive singular, but for the nominative or objective plural. Thus we find such authors as Addison and Swift, writing *Jacobus's* and *genius's*, for *Jacobuses* and *geniuses*; *idea's*, *toga's*, and *tunica's*, for *ideas*, *togas*, and *tunicas*; *enamorato's* and *virtuoso's*, for *enamoratoes* and *virtuosoes*. Errors of this kind, should be carefully avoided.

OBS. 22.—The apostrophe and *s* are sometimes added to mere characters, to denote plurality, and not the possessive case; as, two *a*'s, three *b*'s, four 9's. These we cannot avoid, except by using the *names* of the things: as, two *Aes*, three *Bees*, four *Nines*. "Laced down the sides with little *c*'s."—*Steele*. "Whenever two *gg*'s come together, they are both hard."—*Buchanan*. The names of *c* and *g*, plural, are *Cees* and *Gees*. Did these authors *know* the words, or did they not? To have learned the *names* of the letters, will be found on many occasions a great convenience, especially to critics. For example: "The pronunciation of these two consecutive *s's* is hard."—*Webber's Gram.*, p. 21. Better: "*Esses.*" "*S* and *x*, however, are exceptions. They are pluralyzed by adding *es* preceded by a hyphen [-], as the *s-es*; the *x-es.*"—*O. B. Peirce's Gram.*, p. 40. Better, use the *names, Ess* and *Ex*, and pluralize thus: "the *Esses*; the *Exes.*"

"Make Q's of answers, to waylay
What th' other party's like to say."
　　—*Hudibras*, P. III, C. ii, l. 951.

Here the cipher is to be read *Kues*, but it has not the meaning of this name merely. It is put either for the plural of *Q.*, a *Question*, like D. D.'s, (read *Dee-Dees*,) for *Doctors of Divinity*; or else, more erroneously, for *cues*, the plural of *cue*, a turn which the next speaker catches.

OBS. 23.—In the following example, the apostrophe and *s* are used to give the sound of a *verb's* termination, to words which the writer supposed were not properly verbs: "When a man in a soliloquy reasons with himself, and *pro's* and *con's*, and weighs all his designs."—*Congreve*. But here, "*proes* and *cons*," would have been more accurate. "We put the ordered number of *m's* into our composing-stick."—*Printer's Gram.* Here "*Ems*" would have done as well. "All measures for *folio's* and *quarto's*, should be made to *m's* of the English body; all measures for *octavo's*, to Pica *m's.*"—*Ibid.* Here regularity requires, "*folios, quartoes, octavoes*," and "*pica Ems.*" The verb *is*, when contracted, sometimes gives to its nominative the same form as that of the possessive case, it not being always spaced off for distinction, as it may be; as,

"A *wit's* a feather, and a chief a rod;
An honest *man's* the noblest work of God."
　　—*Pope, on Man*, Ep. iv, l. 247.

OBS. 24.—As the *objective case of nouns* is to be distinguished from the nominative, only by the sense, relation, and position, of words in a sentence, the learner must acquire a habit of attending to these several things. Nor ought it to be a hardship to any reader to understand that which he thinks worth reading. It is seldom possible to mistake one of these cases for the other, without a total misconception of the author's meaning. The nominative denotes the agent, actor, or doer; the person or thing that is made the subject of an affirmation, negation, question, or supposition: its place, except in a question, is commonly *before* the verb. The objective, when governed by a verb or a participle, denotes the person on whom, or the thing on which, the action falls and terminates: it is commonly placed *after* the verb, participle, or preposition, which governs it. Nouns, then, by changing places, may change cases: as, "*Jonathan* loved *David*;" "*David* loved *Jonathan*." Yet the case depends not entirely upon position; for any order in which the words cannot be misunderstood, is allowable: as, "Such tricks hath strong imagination."—*Shak.* Here the cases are known, because the meaning is plainly this: "Strong imagination hath such tricks." "To him give all the prophets witness."—*Acts*, x, 43. This is intelligible enough, and more forcible than the same meaning expressed thus: "All the prophets give witness to him." The *order* of the words never can affect the explanation to be given of them in parsing, unless it change the sense, and form them into a different sentence.

THE DECLENSION OF NOUNS.

The declension of a noun is a regular arrangement of its numbers and cases. Thus:—

EXAMPLE I.—FRIEND.

   Sing. Nom. friend, Plur. Nom. friends,
    Poss. friend's, Poss. friends',
    Obj. friend; Obj. friends.

EXAMPLE II.—MAN.

   Sing. Nom. man, Plur. Nom. men,
    Poss. man's, Poss. men's,
    Obj. man; Obj. men.

EXAMPLE III.—FOX.

   Sing. Nom. fox, Plur. Nom. foxes,
    Poss. fox's, Poss. foxes',
    Obj. fox; Obj. foxes.

EXAMPLE IV.—FLY.

   Sing. Nom. fly, Plur. Nom. flies,
    Poss. fly's, Poss. flies',

Obj. fly; Obj. flies.

EXAMPLES FOR PARSING.

PRAXIS III.—ETYMOLOGICAL.

_In the Third Praxis, it is required of the pupil—to distinguish and define the different parts of speech, and the classes and modifications of the ARTICLES and NOUNS.

The definitions to be given in the Third Praxis, are two for an article, six for a noun, and one for an adjective, a pronoun, a verb, a participle, an adverb, a conjunction, a preposition, or an interjection. Thus_:—

EXAMPLE PARSED.

"The writings of Hannah More appear to me more praiseworthy than Scott's."

The is the definite article. 1. An article is the word *the, an*, or *a*, which we put before nouns to limit their signification. 2. The definite article is *the*, which denotes some particular thing or things.

Writings is a common noun, of the third person, plural number, neuter gender, and nominative case. 1. A noun is the name of any person, place, or thing, that can be known or mentioned. 2. A common noun is the name of a sort, kind, or class, of beings or things. 3. The third person is that which denotes the person or thing merely spoken of. 4. The plural number is that which denotes more than one. 5. The neuter gender is that which denotes things that are neither male nor female. 6. The nominative case is that form or state of a noun or pronoun, which usually denotes the subject of a finite verb.

Of is a preposition. 1. A preposition is a word used to express some relation of different things or thoughts to each other, and is generally placed before a noun or a pronoun.

Hannah More is a proper noun, of the third person, singular number, feminine gender, and objective case. 1. A noun is the name of any person, place, or thing, that can be known or mentioned. 2. A proper noun is the name of some particular individual, or people, or group. 3. The third person is that which denotes the person or thing merely spoken of. 4. The singular number is that which denotes but one. 5. The feminine gender is that which denotes persons or animals of the female kind. 6. The objective case is that form or state of a noun or pronoun, which usually denotes the object of a verb, participle, or preposition.

Appear is a verb. 1. A verb is a word that signifies *to be, to act,* or *to be acted upon.*

To is a preposition. 1. A preposition is a word used to express some relation of different things or thoughts to each other, and is generally placed before a noun or a pronoun.

Me is a pronoun. 1. A pronoun is a word used in stead of a noun.

More is an adverb. 1. An adverb is a word added to a verb, a participle, an adjective, or an other adverb; and generally expresses time, place, degree, or manner.

Praiseworthy is an adjective. 1. An adjective is a word added to a noun or pronoun, and generally expresses quality.

Than is a conjunction. 1. A conjunction is a word used to connect words or sentences in construction, and to show the dependence of the terms so connected.

Scott's is a proper noun, of the third person, singular number, masculine gender, and possessive case. 1. A noun is the name of any person, place, or thing, that can be known or mentioned. 2. A proper noun is the name of some particular individual, or people, or group. 3. The third person is that which denotes the person or thing merely spoken of. 4. The singular number is that which denotes but one. 5. The masculine gender is that which denotes persons or animals of the male kind. 6. The possessive case is that form or state of a noun or pronoun, which usually denotes the relation of property.

LESSON I.—PARSING.

"The virtue of Alexander appears to me less vigorous than that of Socrates. Socrates in Alexander's place I can readily conceive: Alexander in that of Socrates I cannot. Alexander will tell you, he can subdue the world: it was a greater work in Socrates to fulfill the duties of life. Worth consists most, not in great, but in good actions."—*Kames's Art of Thinking*, p. 70.

"No one should ever rise to speak in public, without forming to himself a just and strict idea of what suits his own age and character; what suits the subject, the hearers, the place, the occasion."—*Blair's Rhetoric*, p. 260.

"In the short space of little more than a century, the Greeks became such statesmen, warriors, orators, historians, physicians, poets, critics, painters, sculptors, architects, and, last of all, philosophers, that one can hardly help considering that golden period, as a providential event in honour of human nature, to show to what perfection the species might ascend."—*Harris's Hermes*, p. 417.

"Is genius yours? Be yours a glorious end,
Be your king's, country's, truth's, religion's friend."—*Young.*

LESSON II.—PARSING.

"He that is called in the Lord, being a servant, is the Lord's freeman: likewise also, he that is called, being free, is Christ's servant."—*1 Cor.*, vii, 22.

"What will remain to the Alexanders, and the Cæsars, and the Jenghizes, and the Louises, and the Charleses, and the Napoleons, with whose 'glories' the idle voice of fame is filled?"—*J. Dymond.* "Good sense, clear ideas, perspicuity of language, and proper arrangement of words and thoughts, will always command attention."—*Blair's Rhet.*, p. 174.

"A mother's tenderness and a father's care are nature's gifts for man's advantage.—Wisdom's precepts form the good man's interest and happiness."—*Murray's Key*, p. 194.

"A dancing-school among the Tuscaroras, is not a greater absurdity than a masquerade in America. A theatre, under the best regulations, is not essential to our happiness. It may afford entertainment to individuals; but it is at the expense of private taste and public morals."—*Webster's Essays*, p. 86.

"Where dancing sunbeams on the waters played,
And verdant alders form'd a quivering shade."—*Pope.*

LESSON III.—PARSING.

"I have ever thought that advice to the young, unaccompanied by the routine of honest employments, is like an attempt to make a shrub grow in a certain direction, by blowing it with a bellows."—*Webster's Essays*, p. 247.

"The Arabic characters for the writing of numbers, were introduced into Europe by Pope Sylvester II, in the eleventh century."—*Constable's Miscellany.*

"Emotions raised by inanimate objects, trees, rivers, buildings, pictures, arrive at perfection almost instantaneously; and they have a long endurance, a second view producing nearly the same pleasure with the first."—*Kames's Elements*, i, 108.

"There is great variety in the same plant, by the different appearances of its stem, branches, leaves, blossoms, fruit, size, and colour; and yet, when we trace that variety through different plants, especially of the same kind, there is discovered a surprising uniformity."—*Ib.*, i, 273.

"Attitude, action, air, pause, start, sigh, groan,
He borrow'd, and made use of as his own."—*Churchill.*

"I dread thee, fate, relentless and severe,
With all a poet's, husband's, father's fear!"—*Burns.*

IMPROPRIETIES FOR CORRECTION.

ERRORS OF NOUNS.

LESSON I.—NUMBERS.

"All the ablest of the Jewish Rabbis acknowledge it."—*Wilson's Heb. Gram.*, p. 7.

[FORMULE.—Not proper, because the word *Rabbi* is here made plural by the addition of *s* only. But, according to Observation 12th on the Numbers, nouns in *i* ought rather to form the plural in *ies*. The capital *R*, too, is not necessary. Therefore, *Rabbis* should be *rabbies*, with *ies* and a small *r*.]

"Who has thoroughly imbibed the system of one or other of our Christian rabbis."—*Campbell's Rhet.*, p. 378. "The seeming singularitys of reason soon wear off."—*Collier's Antoninus*, p. 47. "The chiefs and arikis or priests have the power of declaring a place or object taboo."—*Balbi's Geog.*, p. 460. "Among the various tribes of this family, are the Pottawatomies, the Sacs and Foxes, or Saukis and Ottogamis."—*Ib.*, p. 178. "The Shawnees, Kickapoos, Menomonies, Miamis and Delawares, are of the same region."—*Ib.*, p. 178. "The Mohegans and Abenaquis belonged also to this family."—*Ib.*, p. 178. "One tribe of this family, the Winnebagos, formerly resided near lake Michigan."—*Ib.*, p. 179. "The other tribes are the Ioways, the Otoes, the Missouris, the Quapaws."—*Ib.*, p. 179. "The great Mexican family comprises the Aztecs, Toltecs, and Tarascos."—*Ib.*, p. 179. "The Mulattoes are born of negro and white parents; the Zambos, of Indians and negroes."—*Ib.*, p. 165. "To have a place among the Alexanders, the Cæsars, the Lewis', or the Charles', the scourges and butchers of their fellow-creatures."—*Burgh's Dignity*, i, 132. "Which was the notion of the Platonic Philosophers and Jewish rabbii."—*Ib.*, p. 248. "That they should relate to the whole body of virtuosos."—*Gobbett's E. Gram.*, ¶ 212. "What thank have ye? for sinners also love those that love them."—*Luke*, vi, 32. "There are five ranks of nobility; dukes, marquesses, earls, viscounts, and barons."—*Balbi's Geog.*, p. 228. "Acts, which were so well known to the two Charles's."—*Payne's Geog.*, ii, 511. "Court Martials are held in all parts, for the trial of the blacks."—*Observer*, No. 458. "It becomes a common noun, and may have a plural number; as, the two *Davids*; the two *Scipios*, the two *Pompies*."—*Staniford's Gram.*, p. 8. "The food of the rattlesnake is birds, squirrels, hare, rats, and reptiles."—*Balbi's Geog.*, p. 177. "And let fowl multiply in the earth."—*Genesis*, i, 22. "Then we reached the hill-side where eight buffalo were grazing."—*Martineau's Amer.*, i, 202. "*Corset, n.* a pair of bodice for a woman."—*Worcester's Dict.*, 12mo. "As the *be's*; the *ce's*, the *doubleyu's*."—*O. B. Peirce's Gram.*, p. 40. "Simplicity is the means between ostentation and rusticity."—*Pope's Pref. to Homer.* "You have disguised yourselves like tipstaves."—*Gil Blas*, i, 111. "But who, that hath any taste, can endure the incessant quick returns of the *also*'s, and the *likewise*'s, and the *moreover*'s, and the *however*'s, and the *notwithstanding*'s?"—*Campbell's Rhet.*, p. 439.

"Sometimes, in mutual sly disguise,
Let Aye's seem No's, and No's seem Aye's."—*Gay*, p. 431.

LESSON II.—CASES.

"For whose name sake, I have been made willing."—*Wm. Penn.*

[FORMULE.—Not proper, because the noun *name*, which is here meant for the possessive case singular, has not the true form of that case. But, according to a principle on page 258th, "The possessive case of nouns is formed, in the singular number, by adding to the nominative *s preceded by an apostrophe*; and, in the plural, when the nominative ends in *s*, by adding *an apostrophe only*." Therefore, name should be *name's*; thus, "For whose *name's* sake, I have been made willing."]

"Be governed by your conscience, and never ask anybodies leave to be honest."—*Collier's Antoninus*, p. 105. "To overlook nobodies merit or misbehaviour."—*Ib.*, p. 9. "And Hector at last fights his way to the stern of Ajax' ship."—*Coleridge's Introd.*, p. 91. "Nothing is lazier, than to keep ones eye upon words without heeding their meaning."— *Philological*

Museum, i, 645. "Sir William Joneses division of the day."—*Ib.*, *Contents*. "I need only refer here to Vosses excellent account of it."—*Ib.*, i, 465. "The beginning of Stesichoruses palinode has been preserved."—*Ib.*, i, 442. "Though we have Tibulluses elegies, there is not a word in them about Glycera."—*Ib.*, p. 446. "That Horace was at Thaliarchuses country-house."—*Ib.*, i, 451. "That Sisyphuses foot-tub should have been still in existence."—*Ib.*, i, 468. "How every thing went on in Horace's closet, and in Mecenases antechamber."—*Ib.*, i, 458. "Who, for elegant brevities sake, put a participle for a verb."—*Walker's Particles*, p. 42. "The countries liberty being oppressed, we have no more to hope."—*Ib.*, p. 73. "A brief but true account of this peoples' principles."—*Barclay's Pref.* "As, the Churche's Peace, or the Peace of the Church; Virgil's Eneid, or the Eneid of Virgil"—*British Gram.*, p. 93. "As, Virgil's Æneid, for the Æneid of Virgil; the Church'es Peace, for the Peace of the Church."—*Buchanan's Syntax*, p. 18. "Which, with Hubner's Compend, and Wells' Geographia Classica, will be sufficient."— *Burgh's Dignity*, i, 155. "Witness Homer's speaking horses, scolding goddesses, and Jupiter enchanted with Venus' girdle."—*Ib.*, i, 184. "Dr. Watts' Logic may with success be read and commented on to them."—*Ib.*, p. 156. "Potter's Greek, and Kennet's Roman Antiquities, Strauchius' and Helvicus' Chronology."—*Ib.*, p. 161. "*Sing.* Alice' friends, Felix' property; *Plur.* The Alices' friends, The Felixes' property."—*O. B. Peirce's Gram.*, p. 46. "Such as Bacchus'es company,"—"at Bacchus'es festivals."—*Ainsworth's Dict., w. Thyrsus.* "Burn's inimitable *Tam o'Shanter* turns entirely upon such a circumstance."—*Scott's Lay, Notes*, p. 201. "Nominative, Men. Genitive, Mens. Objective, Men."—*Cutler's Gram.*, p. 20. "Mens Happiness or Misery is most part of their own making."—*Locke, on Education*, p. 1. "That your Sons Cloths be never made strait, especially about the Breast."—*Ib.*, p. 15. "Childrens Minds are narrow and weak."—*Ib.*, p. 297. "I would not have little Children much tormented about Punctilio's, or Niceties of Breeding."—*Ib.*, p. 90. "To fill his Head with suitable Idea's."—*Ib.*, p. 113. "The Burgusdiscius's and the Scheiblers did not swarm in those Days, as they do now."—*Ib.*, p. 163. "To see the various ways of dressing—a calve's head!"—*Shenstone*, Brit. Poets, Vol. vii, p. 143.

"He puts it on, and for decorum sake
Can wear it e'en as gracefully as she."—*Cowper's Task*.

LESSON III.—MIXED.

"Simon the witch was of this religion too."—*Bunyan's P. P.*, p. 123.

[FORMULE.—Not proper, because the feminine name *witch* is here applied to a man. But, according to the doctrine of genders, on page 254th, "Names of males are masculine; names of females, feminine;" &c. Therefore, *witch* should be *wizard*; thus, "Simon the *wizard*," &c.]

"Mammodis, n. Coarse, plain India muslins."—*Webster's Dict.* "Go on from single persons to families, that of the Pompeyes for instance."—*Collier's Antoninus*, p. 142. "By which the ancients were not able to account for phænomenas."—*Bailey's Ovid*, p. vi. "After this I married a wife who had lived at Crete, but a Jew by birth."—*Josephus's Life*, p. 194. "The very heathen are inexcusable for not worshipping him."—*Student's Manual*, p. 328. "Such poems as Camoen's Lusiad, Voltaire's Henriade, &c."—*Blair's Rhet.*, p. 422. "My learned correspondent writes a word in defence of large scarves."—SPECT.: in *Joh. Dict.* "The forerunners of an apoplexy are dulness, vertigos, tremblings."—ARBUTHNOT: *ib.* "*Vertigo* changes the *o* into ~*in=es*, making the plural *vertig~in=es*."—*Churchill's Gram.*, p. 59. "*Noctambulo* changes the *o* into =*on=es*, making the plural *noctambul=on=es*."—*Ib.*, p. 59. "What shall we say of noctambulos?"—ARBUTHNOT: *in Joh. Dict.* "In the curious fretwork of rocks and grottos."—*Blair's Rhet.*, p. 220. "*Wharf* makes the plural *wharves*."—

Smith's Gram., p. 45; *Merchant's*, 29; *Picket's*, 21; *Frost's*, 8. "A few cent's worth of maccaroni supplies all their wants."—*Balbi's Geog.*, p. 275. "C sounds hard, like *k*, at the end of a word or syllables."—*Blair's Gram.*, p. 4. "By which the virtuosi try The magnitude of every lie."—*Hudibras.* "Quartos, octavos, shape the lessening pyre."—*Pope's Dunciad*, B. i, l. 162. "Perching within square royal rooves."—SIDNEY: *in Joh. Dict.* "Similies should, even in poetry, be used with moderation."—*Blair's Rhet.*, p. 166. "Similies should never be taken from low or mean objects."—*Ib.*, p. 167. "It were certainly better to say, 'The house of lords,' than 'the Lord's house.'"—*Murray's Gram.*, 8vo, p. 177. "Read your answers. Unit figure? 'Five.' Ten's? 'Six.' Hundreds? 'Seven.'"—*Abbott's Teacher*, p. 79. "Alexander conquered Darius' army."—*Kirkham's Gram.*, p. 58. "Three days time was requisite, to prepare matters."—*Brown's Estimate*, ii, 156. "So we say that Ciceros stile and Sallusts, were not one, nor Cesars and Livies, nor Homers and Hesiodus, nor Herodotus and Theucidides, nor Euripides and Aristophanes, nor Erasmus and Budeus stiles."—*Puttenham's Arte of English Poesie*, iii, 5. "*Lex* (i.e. *legs*) is no other than our ancestors past participle *læg, laid down.*"—*Tooke's Diversions*, ii, 7. "Achaia's sons at Ilium slain for the Atridæ' sake."—*Cowper's Iliad.* "The corpse[167] of half her senate manure the fields of Thessaly."—*Addison's Cato.*

"Poisoning, without regard of fame or fear:
And spotted corpse are frequent on the bier."—*Dryden.*

ADJECTIVES.

An Adjective is a word added to a noun or pronoun, and generally expresses quality: as, A *wise* man; a *new* book. You *two* are *diligent*.

OBSERVATIONS.

OBS. 1.—Adjectives have been otherwise called attributes, attributives, qualities, adnouns; but none of these names is any better than the common one. Some writers have classed adjectives with verbs; because, with a neuter verb for the copula, they often form logical predicates: as, "Vices *are contagious*." The Latin grammarians usually class them with nouns; consequently their nouns are divided into nouns substantive and nouns adjective. With us, substantives are nouns; and adjectives form a part of speech by themselves. This is generally acknowledged to be a much better distribution. Adjectives cannot with propriety be called *nouns*, in any language; because they are not *the names* of the qualities which they signify. They must be *added* to nouns or pronouns in order to make sense. But if, in a just distribution of words, the term "*adjective nouns*" is needless and improper, the term "*adjective pronouns*" is, certainly, not less so: most of the words which Murray and others call by this name, are not pronouns, but adjectives.

OBS. 2.—The noun, or substantive, is a *name*, which makes sense of itself. The adjective is an adjunct to the noun or pronoun. It is a word added to denote quality, situation, quantity, number, form, tendency, or whatever else may characterize and distinguish the thing or things spoken of. Adjectives, therefore, are distinguished *from* nouns by their *relation to* them; a relation corresponding to that which qualities bear to things: so that no part of speech is more easily discriminated than the adjective. Again: English adjectives, as such, are all indeclinable. When, therefore, any words usually belonging to this class, are found to take either the plural or the possessive form, like substantive nouns, they are to be parsed as nouns. To abbreviate expression, we not unfrequently, in this manner, convert adjectives into nouns. Thus, in grammar, we often speak of *nominatives, possessives,* or *objectives,* meaning nouns or pronouns of the nominative, the possessive, or the objective case; of *positives, comparatives,* or *superlatives,* meaning adjectives of the positive, the comparative, or the superlative degree; of *infinitives, subjunctives,* or *imperatives,* meaning verbs of the infinitive, the subjunctive, or the imperative mood; and of *singulars, plurals,* and many other such things, in the same way. So a man's *superiors* or *inferiors* are persons superior or inferior to himself. His *betters* are persons better than he. *Others* are any persons or things distinguished from some that are named or referred to; as, "If you want enemies, excel *others*; if you want friends, let *others* excel you."—*Lacon.* All adjectives thus taken substantively, become *nouns,* and ought to be parsed as such, unless this word *others* is to be made an exception, and called a "*pronoun.*"

"Th' event is fear'd; should we again provoke
Our *stronger,* some worse way his wrath may find."
—*Milton, P. L.,* B. ii, l. 82.

OBS. 3.—Murray says, "Perhaps the words *former* and *latter* may be properly ranked amongst the demonstrative pronouns, *especially in many of their applications.* The following sentence may serve as an example: 'It was happy for the state, that Fabius continued in the command with Minutius: the *former's* phlegm was a check upon the *latter's* vivacity.'"—*Gram.*, 8vo, p. 57. This I take to be bad English. *Former* and *latter* ought to be adjectives only; except when *former* means *maker*. And, if not so, it is too easy a way of multiplying pronouns, to manufacture two out of one single anonymous sentence. If it were said, "The deliberation of *the former* was a seasonable chock upon the fiery temper of *the latter*" the words *former* and *latter* would seem to me not to be pronouns, but adjectives, each relating to the noun *commander* understood after it.

OBS. 4.—The sense and relation of words in sentences, as well as their particular form and meaning, must be considered in parsing, before the learner can say, with certainty, to what class they belong. Other parts of speech, and especially nouns and participles, by a change in their construction, may become adjectives. Thus, to denote the material of which a thing is formed, we very commonly make the name of the substantive an adjective to that of the thing: as, A *gold chain*, a *silver spoon*, a *glass pitcher*, a *tin basin*, an *oak plank*, a *basswood slab*, a *whalebone rod*. This construction is in general correct, whenever the former word may be predicated of the latter; as, "The chain is gold."—"The spoon is silver." But we do not write *gold beater* for *goldbeater*, or *silver smith* for *silversmith*; because the beater is not gold, nor is the smith silver. This principle, however, is not universally observed; for we write *snowball*, *whitewash*, and many similar compounds, though the ball is snow and the wash is white; and *linseed oil*, or *Newark cider*, may be a good phrase, though the former word cannot well be predicated of the latter. So in the following examples: "Let these *conversation* tones be the foundation of public pronunciation."—*Blair's Rhet.*, p. 334. "A *muslin* flounce, made very full, would give a very agreeable *flirtation* air."—POPE: *Priestley's Gram.*, p. 79.

"Come, calm Content, serene and sweet,
O gently guide my *pilgrim* feet
To find thy *hermit* cell."—*Barbauld.*

OBS. 5.—Murray says, "Various nouns placed before other nouns assume the nature of adjectives: as, sea fish, wine vessel, corn field, meadow ground, &c."—*Octavo Gram.*, p. 48. This is, certainly, very lame instruction. If there is not palpable error in all his examples, the propriety of them all is at least questionable; and, to adopt and follow out their principle, would be, to tear apart some thousands of our most familiar compounds. "*Meadow ground*" may perhaps be a correct phrase, since the ground is meadow; it seems therefore preferable to the compound word meadow-ground. What he meant by "*wine vessel*" is doubtful: that is, whether a ship or a cask, a flagon or a decanter. If we turn to our dictionaries, Webster has *sea-fish* and *wine-cask* with a hyphen, and *cornfield* without; while Johnson and others have *corn-field* with a hyphen, and *seafish* without. According to the rules for the figure of words, we ought to write them *seafish, winecask, cornfield.* What then becomes of the thousands of "adjectives" embraced in the "&c." quoted above?

OBS. 6.—The pronouns *he* and *she,* when placed before or prefixed to nouns merely to denote their gender, appear to be used adjectively; as, "The male or *he* animals offered in sacrifice."—*Wood's Dict., w. Males.* "The most usual term is *he* or *she, male* or *female,* employed as an adjective: as, a *he bear,* a *she bear*; a *male elephant,* a *female elephant.*"—*Churchill's Gram.,* p. 69. Most writers, however, think proper to insert a hyphen in the terms here referred to: as, *he-bear, she-bear,* the plurals of which are *he-bears* and *she-bears.* And, judging by the foregoing rule of predication, we must assume that this practice only is right. In the first example, the word *he* is useless; for the term "*male animals*" is sufficiently clear without it. It has been shown in the third chapter, that *he* and *she* are sometimes used as nouns; and that, as such, they may take the regular declension of nouns, making the plurals *hes* and *shes*. But whenever these words are used adjectively to denote gender, whether we choose to insert the hyphen or not, they are, without question, indeclinable, like other adjectives. In the following example, Sanborn will have *he* to be a noun in the *objective* case; but I consider it rather, to be an adjective, signifying *masculine*:

"(*Philosophy*, I say, and call *it He*;
For, whatsoe'er the painter's fancy be,
It a male-virtue seems to me.")—*Cowley*, Brit. Poets, Vol. ii, p. 54.

OBS. 7.—Though verbs give rise to many adjectives, they seldom, if ever, become such by a mere change of construction. It is mostly by assuming an additional termination, that any verb is formed into an adjective: as in *teachable, moveable, oppressive, diffusive, prohibitory*. There are, however, about forty words ending in *ate*, which, without difference of form, are either verbs or adjectives; as, *aggregate, animate, appropriate, articulate, aspirate, associate, complicate, confederate, consummate, deliberate, desolate, effeminate, elate, incarnate, intimate, legitimate, moderate, ordinate, precipitate, prostrate, regenerate, reprobate, separate, sophisticate, subordinate*. This class of adjectives seems to be lessening. The participials in *ed*, are superseding some of them, at least in popular practice: as, *contaminated*, for *contaminate*, defiled; *reiterated*, for *reiterate*, repeated; *situated*, for *situate*, placed; *attenuated*, for *attenuate*, made thin or slender. *Devote, exhaust*, and some other verbal forms, are occasionally used by the poets, in lieu of the participial forms, *devoted, exhausted*, &c.

OBS. 8.—Participles, which have naturally much resemblance to this part of speech, often drop their distinctive character, and become adjectives. This is usually the case whenever they stand immediately *before* the nouns to which they relate; as, A *pleasing* countenance, a *piercing* eye, an *accomplished* scholar, an *exalted* station. Many participial adjectives are derivatives formed from participles by the negative prefix *un*, which reverses the meaning of the primitive word; as, *undisturbed, undivided, unenlightened*. Most words of this kind differ of course from participles, because there are no such verbs as *to undisturb, to undivide*, &c. Yet they may be called participial adjectives, because they have the termination, and embrace the form, of participles. Nor should any participial adjective be needlessly varied from the true orthography of the participle: a distinction is, however, observed by some writers, between *past* and *passed, staid* and *stayed*; and some old words, as *drunken, stricken, shotten, rotten*, now obsolete as participles, are still retained as adjectives. This sort of words will be further noticed in the chapter on participles.

OBS. 9.—Adverbs are generally distinguished from adjectives, by the form, as well as by the construction, of the words. Yet, in instances not a few, the same word is capable of being used both adjectively and adverbially. In these cases, the scholar must determine the part of speech, by the construction alone; remembering that adjectives belong to nouns or pronouns only; and adverbs, to verbs, participles, adjectives, or other adverbs, only. The following examples from Scripture, will partially illustrate this point, which will be noticed again under the head of syntax: "Is your father well?"—*Gen.*, xliii, 27. "Thou hast well said."—*John*, iv, 17. "He separateth very friends."—*Prov.*, xvii, 9. "Esaias is *very* bold."—*Rom.*, x, 20. "For a pretence, ye make *long* prayer."—*Matt.*, xxiii, 14. "They that tarry *long* at the wine."—*Prov.*, xxiii, 30. "It had not *much* earth."—*Mark*, iv, 5. "For she loved *much*."—*Luke*, vii, 47.

OBS. 10.—Prepositions, in regard to their *construction*, differ from adjectives, almost exactly as active-transitive participles differ syntactically from adjectives: that is, in stead of being mere adjuncts to the words which follow them, they govern those words, and refer back to some other term; which, in the usual order of speech, stands before them. Thus, if I say, "A spreading oak," *spreading* is an adjective relating to oak; if, "A boy spreading hay," *spreading* is a participle, governing *hay*, and relating to *boy*, because the boy is the agent of the action. So, when Dr. Webster says, "The *off* horse in a team," *off* is an adjective, relating to the noun *horse*; but, in the phrase, "A man *off* his guard," *off* is a preposition, showing the relation between *man* and *guard*, and governing the latter. The following are other examples: "From the *above* speculations."—*Harris's Hermes*, p. 194. "An *after* period of life."—MARSHALL: *in Web. Dict.* "With some other of the *after* Judaical rites."—*Right of Tythes*, p. 86. "Whom this *beneath* world doth embrace and hug."—*Shak.* "Especially is *over* exertion made."—*Journal of Lit. Conv.*, p. 119. "To both the *under* worlds."—*Hudibras.* "Please to pay to A. B. the amount of the *within* bill." Whether properly used or not, the words *above, after, beneath, over, under, and within,* are here unquestionably made *adjectives*; yet every scholar knows, that they are generally prepositions, though sometimes adverbs.

CLASSES.

Adjectives may be divided into six classes; namely, *common, proper, numeral, pronominal, participial,* and *compound.*

I. A *common adjective* is any ordinary epithet, or adjective denoting quality or situation; as, *Good, bad, peaceful, warlike—eastern, western, outer, inner.*

II. A *proper adjective* is an adjective formed from a proper name; as, *American, English, Platonic, Genoese.*

III. A *numeral adjective* is an adjective that expresses a definite number; as, *One, two, three, four, five, six,* &c.

IV. A *pronominal adjective* is a definitive word which may either accompany its noun, or represent it understood; as, "*All* join to guard what *each* desires to gain."—*Pope.* That is, "*All men* join to guard what *each man* desires to gain."

V. A *participial adjective* is one that has the form of a participle, but differs from it by rejecting the idea of time; as, "An *amusing* story,"—"A *lying* divination."

VI. A *compound adjective* is one that consists of two or more words joined together, either by the hyphen or solidly: as, *Nut-brown, laughter-loving, four-footed; threefold, lordlike, lovesick.*

OBSERVATIONS.

OBS. 1.—This distribution of the adjectives is no less easy to be applied, than necessary to a proper explanation in parsing. How many adjectives there are in the language, it is difficult to say; none of our dictionaries profess to exhibit all that are embraced in some of the foregoing classes. Of the Common Adjectives, there are probably not fewer than six thousand, exclusive of the common nouns which we refer to this class when they are used adjectively. Walker's Rhyming Dictionary contains five thousand or more, the greater part of which may be readily distinguished by their peculiar endings. Of those which end in *ous,* as *generous,* there are about 850. Of those in *y* or *ly,* as *shaggy, homely,* there are about 550. Of those in *ive,* as *deceptive,* there are about 400. Of those in *al,* as *autumnal,* there are about 550. Of those in *ical,* as *mechanical,* there are about 350. Of those in *able,* as *valuable,* there are about 600. Of those in *ible,* as *credible,* there are about 200. Of those in *ent,* as *different,* there are about 300. Of those in *ant,* as *abundant,* there are about 170. Of those in *less,* as *ceaseless,* there are about 220. Of those in *ful,* as *useful,* there are about 130. Of those in *ory,* as *explanatory,* there are about 200. Of those in *ish,* as *childish,* there are about 100. Of those in *ine,* as *masculine,* there are about 70. Of those in *en,* as *wooden,* there are about 50. Of those in *some,* as *quarrelsome,* there are about 30. These sixteen numbers added together, make 4770.

OBS. 2.—The Proper Adjectives are, in many instances, capable of being converted into declinable nouns: as, *European, a European, the Europeans; Greek, a Greek, the Greeks; Asiatic, an Asiatic, the Asiatics*. But with the words *English, French, Dutch, Scotch, Welsh, Irish*, and in general all such as would acquire an additional syllable in their declension, the case is otherwise. The gentile noun has frequently fewer syllables than the adjective, but seldom more, unless derived from some different root. Examples: *Arabic, an Arab, the Arabs; Gallic, a Gaul, the Gauls; Danish, a Dane, the Danes; Moorish, a Moor, the Moors; Polish, a Pole*, or *Polander, the Poles; Swedish, a Swede, the Swedes; Turkish, a Turk, the Turks*. When we say, *the English, the French, the Dutch, the Scotch, the Welsh, the Irish*, —meaning, *the English people, the French people*, &c., many grammarians conceive that *English, French*, &c., are *indeclinable nouns*. But in my opinion, it is better to reckon them *adjectives*, relating to the noun *men* or *people* understood. For if these words are nouns, so are a thousand others, after which there is the same ellipsis; as when we say, *the good, the great, the wise, the learned*.[168] The principle would involve the inconvenience of multiplying our nouns of the singular form and a plural meaning, indefinitely. If they are nouns, they are, in this sense, plural only; and, in an other, they are singular only. For we can no more say, *an English, an Irish*, or *a French*, for *an Englishman, an Irishman*, or *a Frenchman*; than we can say, *an old, a selfish*, or *a rich*, for *an old man, a selfish man*, or *a rich man*. Yet, in distinguishing the *languages*, we call them *English, French, Dutch, Scotch, Welsh, Irish*; using the words, certainly, in no plural sense; and preferring always the line of adjectives, where the gentile noun is different: as, *Arabic*, and not *Arab*; *Danish*, and not *Dane*; *Swedish*, and not *Swede*. In this sense, as well as in the former, Webster, Chalmers, and other modern lexicographers, call the words *nouns*; and the reader will perceive, that the objections offered before do not apply here. But Johnson, in his two quarto volumes, gives only two words of this sort, *English* and *Latin*; and both of these he calls *adjectives*: "ENGLISH, *adj.* Belonging to England; hence English[169] is the language of England." The word *Latin*, however, he makes a noun, when it means a schoolboy's exercise; for which usage he quotes, the following inaccurate example from Ascham: "He shall not use the common order in schools for making of *Latins*."

OBS. 3.—Dr. Webster gives us explanations like these: "CHINESE, *n. sing.* and *plu.* A native of China; also the language of China."—"JAPANESE, *n.* A native of Japan; or the language of the inhabitants."—"GENOESE, *n. pl.* the people of Genoa in Italy. *Addison.*"—"DANISH, *n.* The language of the Danes."—"IRISH, *n.* 1. A native of Ireland. 2. The language of the Irish; the Hiberno-Celtic." According to him, then, it is proper to say, *a Chinese, a Japanese*, or *an Irish*; but not, *a Genoese*, because he will have this word to be plural only! Again, if with him we call a native of Ireland *an Irish*, will not more than one be *Irishes?*[170] If a native of Japan be *a Japanese*, will not more than one be *Japaneses?* In short, is it not plain, that the words, *Chinese, Japanese, Portuguese, Maltese, Genoese, Milanese*, and all others of like formation, should follow one and the same rule? And if so, what is that rule? Is it not this;—that, like *English, French*, &c., they are always *adjectives*; except, perhaps, when they denote *languages*? There may possibly be some real authority from usage, for calling a native of China *a Chinese*,—of Japan *a Japanese*,—&c.; as there is also for the regular plurals, *Chineses, Japaneses*, &c.; but is it, in either case, good and sufficient authority? The like forms, it is acknowledged, are, on some occasions, mere adjectives; and, in modern usage, we do not find these words inflected, as they were formerly. Examples: "The *Chinese* are by no means a cleanly people, either in person or dress."—*Balbi's Geog.*, p. 415. "The *Japanese* excel in working in copper, iron, and steel."—*Ib.*, p. 419. "The *Portuguese* are of the same origin with the Spaniards."—*Ib.*, p. 272. "By whom the undaunted *Tyrolese* are led."—*Wordsworth's Poems*, p. 122.

Again: "Amongst the *Portugueses*, 'tis so much a Fashion, and Emulation, amongst their Children, to *learn* to *Read*, and Write, that they cannot hinder them from it."—*Locke, on Education*, p. 271. "The *Malteses* do so, who harden the Bodies of their Children, and reconcile them to the Heat, by making them go stark Naked."—*Idem, Edition of* 1669, p. 5. "CHINESE, *n. s.* Used elliptically for the language and people of China: plural, *Chineses. Sir T. Herbert.*"—*Abridgement of Todd's Johnson.* This is certainly absurd. For if *Chinese* is used *elliptically* for the people of China, it is an *adjective*, and does not form the plural, *Chineses*: which is precisely what I urge concerning the whole class. These plural forms ought not to be imitated. Horne Tooke quotes some friend of his, as saying, "No, I will never descend with him beneath even *a Japanese*: and I remember what Voltaire remarks of *that country*."—*Diversions of Purley*, i, 187. In this case, he ought, unquestionably, to have said—"beneath even *a native of Japan*;" because, whether *Japanese* be a noun or not, it is absurd to call *a Japanese*, "*that country*." Butler, in his Hudibras, somewhere uses the word *Chineses*; and it was, perhaps, in his day, common; but still, I say, it is contrary to analogy, and therefore wrong. Milton, too, has it:

"But in his way lights on the barren plains
Of Sericana, where Chineses[171] drive
With sails and wind their cany *waggons* light."
    —*Paradise Lost*, B. iii, l. 437.

OBS. 4.—The Numeral Adjectives are of three kinds, namely, *cardinal, ordinal*, and *multiplicative*: each kind running on in a series indefinitely. Thus:—

1. *Cardinal*; One, two, three, four, five, six, seven, eight, nine, ten, eleven, twelve, thirteen, fourteen, fifteen, sixteen, seventeen, eighteen, nineteen, twenty, twenty-one, twenty-two, &c.

2. *Ordinal*; First, second, third, fourth, fifth, sixth, seventh, eighth, ninth, tenth, eleventh, twelfth, thirteenth, fourteenth, fifteenth, sixteenth, seventeenth, eighteenth, nineteenth, twentieth, twenty-first, twenty-second, &c.

3. *Multiplicative*; Single or alone, double or twofold, triple or threefold, quadruple or fourfold, quintuple or fivefold, sextuple or sixfold, septuple or sevenfold, octuple or eightfold, &c. But high terms of this series are seldom used. All that occur above decuple or tenfold, are written with a hyphen, and are usually of round numbers only; as, thirty-fold, sixty-fold, hundred-fold.

OBS. 5.—A cardinal numeral denotes the whole number, but the corresponding ordinal denotes only the last one of that number, or, at the beginning of a series, the first of several or many. Thus: "*One* denotes simply the number *one*, without any regard to more; but *first* has respect to more, and so denotes only the first one of a greater number; and *two* means the number *two* completely; but *second*, the last one of *two*: and so of all the rest."—*Burn's Gram.*, p. 54. A cardinal number answers to the question, "*How many*?" An ordinal number answers to the question, "*Which one*?" or, "*What one*?" All the ordinal numbers, except *first, second, third*, and the compounds of these, as *twenty-first, twenty-second, twenty-third*, are formed directly from the cardinal numbers by means of the termination *th*. And as the primitives, in this case, are many of them either compound words, or phrases consisting of several words, it is to be observed, that the addition is made to the last term only. That is, of every compound ordinal number, the last term only is ordinal in form. Thus we say, *forty-ninth*, and not *fortieth-ninth*; nor could the meaning of the phrase, *four hundred and fiftieth*, be expressed by saying, *fourth hundredth and fiftieth*; for this, if it means any thing, speaks of three different numbers.

OBS. 6.—Some of the numerals are often used as *nouns*; and, as such, are regularly declined: as, *Ones, twoes, threes, fours, fives,* &c. So, *Fifths, sixths, sevenths, eighths, ninths, tenths,* &c. "The *seventy's* translation."—*Wilson's Hebrew Gram.*, p. 32. "I will not do it for *forty's* sake."—*Gen.*, xviii, 29. "I will not destroy it for *twenty's* sake."—*Ib.*, ver. 31. "For *ten's* sake."—*Ib.*, ver. 32. "They sat down in ranks, by *hundreds,* and by *fifties.*"—*Mark,* vi, 40. "There are *millions* of truths that a man is not concerned to know."—*Locke.* With the compound numerals, such a construction is less common; yet the denominator of a fraction may be a number of this sort: as, seven *twenty-fifths.* And here it may be observed, that, in stead of the ancient phraseology, as in 1 Chron., xxiv, 17th, "The *one and twentieth* to Jachin, the *two and twentieth* to Gamul, the *three and twentieth* to Delaiah, the *four and twentieth* to Maaziah," we now generally say, *the twenty-first, the twenty-second,* &c.; using the hyphen in all compounds till we arrive at *one hundred,* or *one hundredth,* and then first introducing the word *and*; as, *one hundred and one,* or *one hundred and first,* &c.

OBS. 7.—The Pronominal Adjectives are comparatively very few; but frequency of use gives them great importance in grammar. The following words are perhaps all that properly belong to this class, and several of these are much oftener something else: *All, any, both, certain, divers, each, either, else, enough, every, few, fewer, fewest, former, first, latter, last, little, less, least, many, more, most, much, neither, no* or *none, one, other, own, only, same, several, some, such, sundry, that, this, these, those, what, whatever, whatsoever, which, whichever, whichsoever.*[172] Of these forty-six words, seven are always singular, if the word *one* is not an exception; namely, *each, either, every, neither, one, that, this*: and nine or ten others are always plural, if the word *many* is not an exception; namely, *both, divers, few, fewer, fewest, many, several, sundry, these, those.* All the rest, like our common adjectives, are applicable to nouns of either number. *Else, every, only, no,* and *none,* are definitive words, which I have thought proper to call pronominal adjectives, though only the last can now with propriety be made to represent its noun understood. "Nor has Vossius, or *any else* that I know of, observed it."—*Johnson's Gram. Com.,* p. 279. Say, "or any *one* else." Dr. Webster explains this word *else* thus: "ELSE, *a.* or *pron.* [Sax. *elles*] Other; one or something *beside*; as, Who *else* is coming?"—*Octavo Dict.* "Each and *every* of them," is an old phrase in which *every* is used pronominally, or with ellipsis of the word to which it refers; but, in common discourse, we now say, *every one, every man,* &c., never using the word *every* alone to suggest its noun. *Only* is perhaps most commonly an adverb; but it is still in frequent use as an adjective; and in old books we sometimes find an ellipsis of the noun to which it belongs; as, "Neither are they the *only* [verbs] in which it is read."—*Johnson's Grammatical Commentaries,* p. 373. "But I think he is the *only* [one] of these Authors."—*Ib.,* p. 193. *No* and *none* seem to be only different forms of the same adjective; the former being used before a noun expressed, and the latter when the noun is understood, or not placed after the adjective; as, "For *none* of us liveth to himself, and *no* man dieth to himself."—*Romans,* xiv, 7. *None* was anciently used for *no* before all words beginning with a vowel sound; as, "They are sottish children; and they have *none* understanding."—*Jeremiah,* iv, 22. This practice is now obsolete. *None* is still used, when its noun precedes it; as,

"Fools! who from hence into the notion fall,
That *vice* or *virtue* there is *none* at all."—*Pope.*

OBS. 8.—Of the words given in the foregoing list as pronominal adjectives, about one third are sometimes used *adverbially.* They are the following: *All,* when it means *totally; any,* for *in any degree; else,* meaning *otherwise; enough,* signifying *sufficiently; first,* for *in the first place; last,* for *in the last place; little,* for *in a small degree; less,* for *in a smaller degree; least,* for *in the smallest degree; much,* for *in a great degree; more,* for *in a greater degree; most,* for *in the greatest degree; no,* or *none,* for *in no degree; only,* for *singly, merely, barely; what,* for *in what degree,* or *in how great a degree.*[173] To these may perhaps be added the word *other,* when used as an alternative to *somehow;* as, "*Somehow* or *other* he will be favoured."—*Butler's Analogy,* p. 89. Here *other* seems to be put for *otherwise;* and yet the latter word would not be agreeable in such a sentence. "*Somewhere or other,*" is a kindred phrase equally common, and equally good; or, rather, equally irregular and puzzling. Would it not be better, always to avoid both, by saying, in their stead, "*In some way or other,*"—"*In someplace or other?*" In the following examples, however, *other* seems to be used for *otherwise,* without such a connection: "How is THAT used, *other* than as a Conjunction?"—*Ainsworth's Gram.,* p. 88.

"Will it not be receiv'd that they have done 't?
—Who dares receive it *other?*"—SHAK.: *Joh. Dict., w. Other.*

OBS. 9.—*All* and *enough, little* and *much, more* and *less,* sometimes suggest the idea of quantity so abstractly, that we can hardly consider them as adjuncts to any other words; for which reason, they are, in this absolute sense, put down in our dictionaries as *nouns.* If nouns, however, they are never inflected by cases or numbers; nor do they in general admit the usual adjuncts or definitives of nouns.[174] Thus, we can neither say, *the all,* for *the whole,* nor *an enough,* for *a sufficiency.* And though *a little, the more,* and *the less,* are common phrases, the article does not here prove the following word to be a noun; because the expression may either be elliptical, or have the construction of an adverb: as, "Though *the more* abundantly I love you, *the less* I be loved."—*2 Cor.,* xii, 15. Dr. Johnson seems to suppose that the partitive use of these words makes them nouns; as, "They have *much of the poetry* of Mecænas, but *little of his liberality.*"—DRYDEN: *in Joh. Dict.* Upon this principle, however, adjectives innumerable would be made nouns; for we can just as well say, "*Some of the poetry*,"—"*Any of the poetry*,"—"*The best of Poetry*," &c. In all such expressions, the name of the thing divided, is understood in the partitive word; for a part of any thing must needs be of the same species as the whole. Nor was this great grammarian sufficiently attentive to adjuncts, in determining the parts of speech. *Nearly all, quite enough, so little, too much, vastly more, rather less*, and an abundance of similar phrases, are familiar to every body; in none of which, can any of these words of quantity, however abstract, be very properly reckoned nouns; because the preceding word is an adverb, and adverbs do not relate to any words that are literally nouns. All these may also be used partitively; as, "*Nearly all of us*."

OBS. 10.—The following are some of Dr. Johnson's "*nouns*;" which, in connexion with the foregoing remarks, I would submit to the judgement of the reader: "'Then shall we be news-crammed.'—'*All* the better; we shall be the more remarkable.'"—SHAK.: *in Joh. Dict.* "*All* the fitter, Lentulus; our coming is not for salutation; we have business."—BEN JONSON: *ib.* "'Tis *enough* for me to have endeavoured the union of my country."—TEMPLE: *ib.* "Ye take too *much* upon you."—NUMBERS: *ib.* "The fate of love is such, that still it sees too *little* or too *much*."—DRYDEN: *ib.* "He thought not *much* to clothe his enemies."—MILTON: *ib.* "There remained not so *much* as one of them."—*Ib., Exod.*, xiv, 28. "We will cut wood out of Lebanon, as *much* as thou shalt need."—*Ib., 2 Chronicles.* "The matter of the universe was created before the flood; if any *more* was created, then there must be as *much* annihilated to make room for it."—BURNET: *ib.* "The Lord do so, and much *more*, to Jonathan."—1 SAMUEL: *ib.* "They that would have *more* and *more*, can never have *enough*; no, not if a miracle should interpose to gratify their avarice."—L'ESTRANGE: *ib.* "They gathered some *more*, some *less*."—EXODUS: *ib.* "Thy servant knew nothing of this, *less* or *more*."—1 SAMUEL: *ib.* The first two examples above, Johnson explains thus: "That is, '*Every thing is the better*.'—*Every thing is the fitter*."—*Quarto Dict.* The propriety of this solution may well be doubted; because the similar phrases, "*So much* the better,"—"*None* the fitter," would certainly be perverted, if resolved in the same way: *much* and *none* are here, very clearly, adverbs.

OBS. 11.—Whatever disposition may be made of the terms cited above, there are instances in which some of the same words can hardly be any thing else than nouns. Thus *all*, when it signifies *the whole*, or *every thing*, may be reckoned a noun; as, "Our *all* is at stake, and irretrievably lost, if we fail of success."—*Addison.* "A torch, snuff and *all*, goes out in a moment, when dipped in the vapour."—*Id.* "The first blast of wind laid it flat on the ground; nest, eagles, and *all*."—*L'Estrange.*

"Finding, the wretched *all* they here can have,
But present food, and but a future grave."—*Prior.*

"And will she yet debase her eyes on me;
On me, whose *all* not equals Edward's moiety?"—*Shak.*

"Thou shalt be *all* in *all*, and I in thee,
Forever; and in me all whom thou lov'st."—*Milton.*

OBS. 12.—There are yet some other words, which, by their construction alone, are to be distinguished from the pronominal adjectives. *Both*, when it stands as a correspondent to *and*, is reckoned a conjunction; as, "For *both* he that sanctifieth, *and* they who are sanctified, are all of one."—*Heb.*, ii, 11. But, in sentences like the following, it seems to be an adjective, referring to the nouns which precede: "Language and manners are *both* established by the usage of people of fashion."—*Amer. Chesterfield*, p. 83. So *either*, corresponding to *or*, and *neither*, referring to *nor*, are conjunctions, and not adjectives. *Which* and *what*, with their compounds, *whichever* or *whichsoever*, *whatever* or *whatsoever*, though sometimes put before nouns as adjectives, are, for the most part, relative or interrogative pronouns. When the noun is used after them, they are adjectives; when it is omitted, they are pronouns: as, "There is a witness of God, *which witness* gives true judgement."—*I. Penington.* Here the word *witness* might be omitted, and *which* would become a relative pronoun. Dr. Lowth says, "*Thy, my, her, our, your, their*, are pronominal adjectives."—*Gram.*, p. 23. This I deny; and the reader may see my reasons, in the observations upon the declension of pronouns.

OBS. 13.—The words *one* and *other*, besides their primitive uses as adjectives, in which they still remain without inflection, are frequently employed as nouns, or as substitutes for nouns; and, in this substantive or pronominal character, they commonly have the regular declension of nouns, and are reckoned such by some grammarians; though others call them indefinite pronouns, and some, (among whom are Lowth and Comly,) leave them with the pronominal adjectives, even when they are declined in both numbers. Each of them may be preceded by either of the articles; and so general is the signification of the former, that almost any adjective may likewise come before it: as, *Any one, some one, such a one, many a one, a new one, an old one, an other one, the same one, the young ones, the little ones, the mighty ones, the wicked one, the Holy One, the Everlasting One.* So, like the French *on*, or *l'on*, the word *one*, without any adjective, is now very frequently used as a general or indefinite term for any man, or any person. In this sense, it is sometimes, unquestionably, to be preferred to a personal pronoun applied indefinitely: as, "Pure religion, and undefiled before God and the Father, is this, To visit the fatherless and widows in their affliction, and to keep *himself* [better, *one's self*] unspotted from the world."—*James*, i, 27. But, as its generality of meaning seems to afford a sort of covering for egotism, some writers are tempted to make too frequent a use of it. Churchill ridicules this practice, by framing, or anonymously citing, the following sentence: "If *one* did but dare to abide by *one's* own judgement, *one's* language would be much more refined; but *one* fancies *one's* self obliged to follow, whereever the many choose to lead *one*."—See *Churchill's Gram.*, p. 229. Here every scholar will concur with the critic in thinking, it would be better to say: "If *we* did but dare to abide by *our* own judgement, *our* language would be much more refined; but *we* fancy *ourselves* obliged to follow wherever the many choose to lead *us*."—See *ib.*

OBS. 14.—Of the pronominal adjectives the following distribution has been made: "*Each, every,* and *either,* are called *distributives*; because, though they imply all the persons or things that make up a number, they consider them, not as one whole, but as taken separately. *This, that, former, latter, both, neither,* are termed *demonstratives*; because they point out precisely the subjects to which they relate. *This* has *these* for its plural; *that* has *those. This* and *that* are frequently put in opposition to each other; *this,* to express what is nearer in place or time; *that,* what is more remote. *All, any, one, other, some, such,* are termed *indefinite. Another* is merely *other* in the singular, with the indefinite article not kept separate from it.[175] *Other,* when not joined with a noun, is occasionally used both in the possessive case, and in the plural number: as,

'Teach me to feel *an other's* wo, to hide the fault I see;
That mercy I to *others* show, that mercy show to me.'—*Pope.*

Each other and *one another,* when used in conjunction, may be termed *reciprocals*; as they are employed to express a reciprocal action; the former, between two persons or things; the latter, *between*[176] more than two. The possessive cases of the personal pronouns have been also ranked under the head of pronominal adjectives, and styled possessives; but for this I see no good reason."—*Churchill's Gram.*, p. 76.

OBS. 15.—The reciprocal terms *each other* and *one an other* divide, according to some mutual act or interchangeable relation, the persons or things spoken of, and are commonly of the singular number only. *Each other*, if rightly used, supposes two, and only two, to be acting and acted upon reciprocally; *one an other*, if not misapplied, supposes more than two, under like circumstances, and has an indefinite reference to all taken distributively: as, "Brutus and Aruns killed *each other*." That is, *Each combatant* killed *the other*. "The disciples were commanded to love *one an other*, and to be willing to wash *one an other's* feet." That is, *All* the disciples were commanded to love *mutually*; for both terms, *one* and *other*, or *one disciple* and *an other disciple*, must be here understood as taken indefinitely. The reader will observe, that the two terms thus brought together, if taken substantively or pronominally in parsing, must be represented as being of *different cases*; or, if we take them adjectively the noun, which is twice to be supplied, will necessarily be so.

OBS. 16.—Misapplications of the foregoing reciprocal terms are very frequent in books, though it is strange that phrases so very common should not be rightly understood. Dr. Webster, among his explanations of the word *other*, has the following: "Correlative to *each*, and applicable to *any number* of individuals."—*Octavo Dict.* "*Other* is used as a substitute for a noun, and in this use has the plural number and the sign of the possessive case."—*Ib.* Now it is plain, that the word *other*, as a "correlative to *each*," may be so far "a substitute for a noun" as to take the form of the possessive case singular, and perhaps also the plural; as, "Lock'd in *each other's* arms they lay." But, that the objective *other*, in any such relation, can convey a plural idea, or be so loosely applicable—"to *any number* of individuals," I must here deny. If it were so, there would be occasion, by the foregoing rule, to make it plural in form; as, "The ambitious strive to excel *each others*." But this is not English. Nor can it be correct to say of more than two, "They all strive to excel *each other*." Because the explanation must be, "*Each* strives to excel *other*;" and such a construction of the word *other* is not agreeable to modern usage. *Each other* is therefore not equivalent to *one an other*, but nearer perhaps to *the one the other*: as, "The two generals are independent *the one of the other*."—*Voltaire's Charles XII*, p. 67. "And these are contrary *the one to the other*."—*Gal.*, v, 17. "The necessary connexion *of the one with the other*."—*Blair's Rhet.*, p. 304. The latter phraseology, being definite and formal, is now seldom used, except the terms be separated by a verb or a preposition. It is a literal version of the French *l'un l'autre*, and in some instances to be preferred to *each other*; as,

"So fellest foes, whose plots have broke their sleep,
To take *the one the other*, by some chance."—*Shak.*

OBS. 17.—The Greek term for the reciprocals *each other* and *one an other*, is a certain plural derivative from [Greek: allos], *other*; and is used in three cases, the genitive, [Greek: allælon], the dative, [Greek: allælois], the accusative, [Greek: allælous]: these being all the cases which the nature of the expression admits; and for all these we commonly use the *objective*;—that is, we put *each* or *one* before the objective *other*. Now these English terms, taken in a reciprocal sense, seldom, if ever, have any plural form; because the article in *one an other* admits of none; and *each other*, when applied to two persons or things, (as it almost always is,) does not require any. I have indeed seen, in some narrative, such an example as this: "The two men were ready to cut *each others' throats*." But the meaning could not be, that each was ready to cut "*others' throats*;" and since, between the two, there was but one throat for *each* to cut, it would doubtless be more correct to say, "*each other's throat*." So Burns, in touching a gentler passion, has an inaccurate elliptical expression:

"'Tis when a youthful, loving, modest pair,
In *others'* arms, breathe out the tender tale."
—*Cotter's Sat. Night.*

He meant, "In *each other's* arms;" the apostrophe being misplaced, and the metre improperly allowed to exclude a word which the sense requires. Now, as to the plural of *each other*, although we do not use the objective, and say of many, "They love *each others*," there appear to be some instances in which the possessive plural, *each others'*, would not be improper; as, "Sixteen ministers, who meet weekly at *each other's* houses."—*Johnson's Life of Swift*. Here the singular is wrong, because the governing noun implies a plurality of owners. "The citizens of different states should know *each others characters*."—*Webster's Essays*, p. 35. This also is wrong, because no possessive sign is used. Either write, "*each others' characters*," or say, "*one an other's character*."

OBS. 18.—*One* and *other* are, in many instances, terms relative and partitive, rather than reciprocal; and, in this use, there seems to be an occasional demand for the plural form. In French, two parties are contrasted by *les uns*—*les autres*; a mode of expression seldom, if ever imitated in English. Thus: "Il les séparera *les uns* d'avec *les autres*." That is, "He shall separate them *some* from *others*;"—or, literally, "*the ones* from *the others*." Our version is: "He shall separate them *one from an other*."—*Matt.*, xxv, 32. Beza has it: "Separabit eos *alteros ab alteris*." The Vulgate: "Separabit eos *ab invicem*." The Greek: "[Greek: Aphoriei autous ap allælon]." To separate many "*one from an other*," seems, literally, to leave none of them together; and this is not, "as a shepherd divideth his sheep from the goats." To express such an idea with perfect propriety, in our language, therefore, we must resort to some other phraseology. In Campbell's version, we read: "And *out of them* he will separate *the good from the bad*, as a shepherd separateth *the* sheep from the goats." Better, perhaps, thus: "And he shall separate them, *the righteous from the wicked*, as a shepherd divideth his sheep from the goats."

OBS. 19.—Dr. Bullions says, "*One* and *other* refer to *the singular only.*"—*Eng. Gram.*, p. 98. Of *ones* and *others* he takes no notice; nor is he sufficiently attentive to usage in respect to the roots. If there is any absurdity in giving a *plural* meaning to the singulars *one* and *other,* the following sentences need amendment: "*The one* preach Christ of contention; but *the other,* of love."—*Philippians*, i, 16. Here "*the one*" is put for "the one *class,*" and "*the other*" for "the other *class;*" the ellipsis in the first instance not being a very proper one. "The confusion arises, when *the one* will put *their* sickle into *the other's* harvest."—LESLEY: *in Joh. Dict.* This may be corrected by saying, "*the one party,*" or, "*the one nation,*" in stead of "*the one.*" "It is clear from Scripture, that Antichrist shall be permitted to work false miracles, and that they shall so counterfeit the true, that it will be hard to discern *the one* from *the other.*"—*Barclay's Works*, iii, 93. If in any ease we may adopt the French construction above, "*the ones* from the *others,*" it will be proper here. Again: "I have seen *children* at a table, who, whatever was there, never asked for any thing, but contentedly took what was given them: and, at an other place, I have seen *others* cry for every thing they saw; they must be served out of every dish, and that first too. What made this vast difference, but this: That *one was* accustomed to have what *they* called or cried for; *the other* to go without it?"—*Locke, on Education*, p. 55. Here, (with *were* for *was,*) the terms of contrast ought rather to have been, *the ones—the others; the latter—the former*; or, *the importunate—the modest.* "Those nice shades, by which *virtues and vices* approach *each one another.*"—*Murray's Gram.*, i, p. 350. This expression should be any thing, rather than what it is. Say, "By which *virtue* and *vice* approach *each other.*" Or: "By which certain virtues and vices *approximate — blend—become difficult of distinction.*"

OBS. 20.—"Most authors have given the name of *pronoun adjectives,* ['pronouns adjective,' or 'pronominal adjectives,'] to *my, mine; our, ours; thy, thine; your, yours; his, her, hers; their, theirs*: perhaps because they are followed by, or refer to, some substantive [expressed or understood after them]. But, were they adjectives, they must either express the quality of their substantive, or limit its extent: adjectives properly so called, do the first; definitive pronouns do the last. All adjectives [that are either singular or plural,] agree with their substantives in *number*; but I can say, 'They are *my books*:' *my* is singular, and *books* plural; therefore *my* is not an adjective. Besides, *my* does not express the *quality* of the books, but only ascertains the possessor, the same as the genitive or substantive does, to which it is similar. Examples: 'They are *my* books;'—'They are *John's* books;' &c."—*Alex. Murray's Gram.*, p. 108.

OBS. 21.—To the class of Participial Adjectives, should be referred all such words as the following: (1.) The simple participles made adjectives by position; as. "A *roaring* lion,"—"A *raging* bear,"—"A *brawling* woman,"—"A *flattering* mouth,"—"An *understanding* heart,"—"*Burning* coals,"—"The *hearing* ear, and the *seeing* eye."—*Bible*. "A *troubled* fountain,"—"A *wounded* spirit,"—"An *appointed* time."—*Ib*. (2.) Words of a participial appearance, formed from nouns by adding *ed*; as, "The eve thy *sainted* mother died."—*W. Scott*. "What you write of me, would make me more *conceited*, than what I scribble myself."—*Pope*. (3.) Participles, or participial adjectives, reversed in sense by the prefix *un*; as, *unaspiring, unavailing, unbelieving, unbattered, uninjured, unbefriended*. (4.) Words of a participial form construed elliptically, as if they were nouns; as, "Among the *dying* and the dead."—"The *called* of Jesus Christ."—*Rom.*, i, 6. "Dearly *beloved*, I beseech you."—*1 Pet.*, ii, 11. "The *redeemed* of the Lord shall return."—*Isaiah*, li, 11. "They talk, to the grief of thy *wounded*."—*Psalms*, lxix, 26: *Margin*.

OBS. 22.—In the text, Prov., vii, 26, "She hath cast down many wounded," *wounded* is a participle; because the meaning is, "*many men wounded*," and not, "*many wounded men*." Our Participial Adjectives are exceedingly numerous. It is not easy to ascertain how many there are of them; because almost any simple participle may be set before a noun, and thus become an adjective: as,

"Where *smiling* spring its earliest visit paid,
And *parting* summer's *ling'ring* blooms delay'd."—*Goldsmith.*

OBS. 23.—Compound Adjectives, being formed at pleasure, are both numerous and various. In their formation, however, certain analogies may be traced: (1.) Many of them are formed by joining an adjective to its noun, and giving to the latter the participial termination *ed*; as, *able-bodied, sharp-sighted, left-handed, full-faced, flat-nosed, thick-lipped, cloven-footed, high-heeled.* (2.) In some, two nouns are joined, the latter assuming *ed*, as above; as, *bell-shaped, hawk-nosed, eagle-sighted, lion-hearted, web-footed.* (3.) In some, the object of an active participle is placed before it; as, *money-getting, time-serving, self-consuming, cloud-compelling, fortune-hunting, sleep-disturbing.* (4.) Some, embracing numerals, form a series, though it is seldom carried far; as, *one-legged, two-legged, three-legged, four-legged.* So, *one-leaved, two-leaved, three-leaved, four-leaved*: or, perhaps better as Webster will have them, *one-leafed, two-leafed, &c.* But, upon the same principle, *short-lived*, should be *short-lifed*, and *long-lived, long-lifed.* (5.) In some, there is a combination of an adjective and a participle; as, *noble-looking, high-sounding, slow-moving, thorough-going, hard-finished, free-born, heavy-laden, only-begotten.* (6.) In some, we find an adverb and a participle united; as, *ever-living, ill-judging, well-pleasing, far-shooting, forth-issuing, back-sliding, ill-trained, down-trodden, above-mentioned.* (7.) Some consist of a noun and a participle which might be reversed with a preposition between them; as, *church-going, care-crazed, travel-soiled, blood-bespotted, dew-sprinkled.* (8.) A few, and those inelegant, terminate with a preposition; as, *unlooked-for, long-looked-for, unthought-of, unheard-of.* (9.) Some are phrases of many words, converted into one part of speech by the hyphen; as, "Where is the *ever-to-be-honoured* Chaucer?"—*Wordsworth*.

"And, with *God-only-knows-how-gotten* light,
Informs the nation what is wrong or right."
—*Snelling's Gift for Scribblers*, p. 49.

OBS. 24.—Nouns derived from compound adjectives, are generally disapproved by good writers; yet we sometimes meet with them: as, *hard-heartedness*, for hardness of heart, or cruelty; *quick-sightedness*, for quickness of sight, or perspicacity; *worldly-mindedness*, for devotion to the world, or love of gain; *heavenly-mindedness*, for the love of God, or true piety. In speaking of ancestors or descendants, we take the noun, *father, mother, son, daughter*, or *child*; prefix the adjective *grand*; for the second generation; *great*, for the, third; and then, sometimes, repeat the same, for degrees more remote: as, *father, grandfather, great-grandfather, great-great-grandfather*. "What would my *great-grandmother* say, thought I, could she know that thou art to be chopped up for fuel to warm the frigid fingers of her *great-great-great-granddaughters*!"—*T. H. Bayley*.

MODIFICATIONS.

Adjectives have, commonly, no modifications but the forms of *comparison*. Comparison is a variation of the adjective, to express quality in different degrees: as, *hard, harder, hardest; soft, softer, softest*.

There are three degrees of comparison; the *positive*, the *comparative*, and the *superlative*.

The *positive degree* is that which is expressed by the adjective in its simple form: as, "An elephant is *large*; a mouse, *small*; a lion, *fierce, active*, *bold,* and *strong.*"

The *comparative degree* is that which is *more* or *less* than something contrasted with it: as, "A whale is *larger* than an elephant; a mouse is a much *smaller* animal than a rat."

The *superlative degree* is that which is *most* or *least* of all included with it: as, "The whale is the *largest* of the animals that inhabit this globe; the mouse is the *smallest* of all beasts."—*Dr. Johnson.*

Those adjectives whose signification does not admit of different degrees, cannot be compared; as, *two, second, all, every, immortal, infinite.*

Those adjectives which may be varied in sense, but not in form, are compared by means of adverbs; as, fruitful, *more* fruitful, *most* fruitful—fruitful, *less* fruitful, *least* fruitful.

OBSERVATIONS.

OBS. 1.—"Some scruple to call the positive a degree of comparison; on the ground, that it does not imply either comparison, or degree. But no quality can exist, without existing in some degree: and, though the positive is very frequently used without reference to any other degree; as it is *the standard,* with which other degrees of the quality are compared, it is certainly an essential object of the comparison. While these critics allow only two degrees, we might in fact with more propriety say, that there are five: 1, the quality in its standard state, or positive degree; as *wise:* 2, in a higher state, or the comparative ascending; *more wise:* 3, in a lower, or the comparative descending; *less wise:* 4, in the highest state, or superlative ascending; *most wise:* 5, in the lowest state, or superlative descending; *least wise.* All grammarians, however, agree about the things themselves, and the forms used to express them; though they differ about the names, by which these forms should be called: and as those names are practically best, which tend least to perplex the learner, I see no good reason here for deviating from what has been established by long custom."—*Churchill's Gram.*, p. 231.

OBS. 2.—Churchill here writes plausibly enough, but it will be seen, both from his explanation, and from the foregoing definitions of the degrees of comparison, that there are but three. The comparative and the superlative may each be distinguishable into the ascending and the descending, as often as we prefer the adverbial form to the regular variation of the adjective itself; but this imposes no necessity of classing and defining them otherwise than simply as the comparative and the superlative. The assumption of two comparatives and two superlatives, is not only contrary to the universal practice of the teachers of grammar; but there is this conclusive argument against it—that the regular method of comparison has no degrees of diminution, and the form which has such degrees, is *no inflection* of the adjective. If there is any exception, it is in the words, *small, smaller, smallest,* and *little, less, least.* But of the smallness or littleness, considered abstractly, these, like all others, are degrees of increase, and not of diminution. *Smaller* is as completely opposite to *less small,* as *wiser* is to *less wise. Less* itself is a comparative descending, only when it diminishes some *other* quality: *less little,* if the phrase were proper, must needs be nearly equivalent to *greater* or *more.* Churchill, however, may be quite right in the following remark: "The comparative ascending of an adjective, and the comparative descending of an adjective expressing the opposite quality, are often considered synonymous, by those who do not discriminate nicely between ideas. But *less imprudent* does not imply precisely the same thing as *more prudent*; or *more brave,* the same as *less cowardly*."—*New Gram.*, p. 231.

OBS. 3.—The definitions which I have given of the three degrees of comparison, are new. In short, I know not whether any other grammarian has ever given what may justly be called a *definition*, of any one of them. Here, as in most other parts of grammar, loose *remarks*, ill-written and untrue assertions, have sufficed. The explanations found in many English grammars are the following: "The positive state expresses the quality of an object, without any increase or diminution; as, good, wise, great. The comparative degree increases or lessens the positive in signification; as, wiser, greater, less wise. The superlative degree increases or lessens the positive to the highest or [the] lowest degree; as, wisest, greatest, least wise. The simple word, or positive, becomes [the] comparative by adding *r* or *er*; and the superlative by adding *st* or *est*, to the end of it. And the adverbs *more* and *most*, placed before the adjective, have the same effect; as, wise, *more* wise, *most* wise."—*Murray's Grammar*, 2d Ed., 1796, p. 47. If a man wished to select some striking example of bad writing—of thoughts ill conceived, and not well expressed—he could not do better than take the foregoing: provided his auditors knew enough of grammar to answer the four simple questions here involved; namely, What is the positive degree? What is the comparative degree? What is the superlative degree? How are adjectives regularly compared? To these questions I shall furnish *direct answers*, which the reader may compare with such as he can derive from the foregoing citation: the last two sentences of which Murray ought to have credited to Dr. Lowth; for he copied them literally, except that he says, "the adverbs *more* AND *most*," for the Doctor's phrase, "the adverbs *more* OR *most*." See the whole also in *Kirkham's Grammar*, p. 72; in *Ingersoll's*, p. 35; in *Alger's*, p. 21; in *Bacon's*, p. 18; in *Russell's*, p. 14; in *Hamlin's*, p. 22; in *J. M. Putnam's*, p. 33; in *S. Putnam's*, p. 20; in *R. C. Smith's*, p. 51; in *Rev. T. Smith's*, p. 20.

OBS. 4.—In the five short sentences quoted above, there are more errors, than can possibly be enumerated in ten times the space. For example: (1.) If one should say of a piece of iron, "It grows cold or hot very rapidly," *cold* and *hot* could not be in the "*positive state*," as they define it: because, either the "quality" or the "object," (I know not which,) is represented by them as "without any increase or diminution;" and this would not, in the present case, be true of either; for iron changes in bulk, by a change of temperature. (2.) What, in the first sentence, is erroneously called "the positive *state*," in the second and the third, is called, "the positive *degree*;" and this again, in the fourth, is falsely identified with "the simple *word*." Now, if we suppose the meaning to be, that "the positive state," "the positive degree," or "the simple word," is "without any increase or diminution;" this is expressly contradicted by three sentences out of the five, and implicitly, by one of the others. (3.) Not one of these sentences is *true*, in the most obvious sense of the words, if in any other; and yet the doctrines they were designed to teach, may have been, in general, correctly gathered from the examples. (4.) The phrase, "*positive in signification*," is not intelligible in the sense intended, without a comma after *positive*; and yet, in an armful of different English grammars which contain the passage, I find not one that has a point in that place. (5.) It is not more correct to say, that the comparative or the superlative degree, "increases or lessens the positive," than it would be to aver, that the plural number increases or lessens the singular, or the feminine gender, the masculine. Nor does the superlative mean, what a certain learned Doctor understands by it—namely, "*the greatest or least possible degree.*" If it did, "the *thickest* parts of his skull," for example, would imply small room for brains; "the *thinnest*," protect them ill, if there were any. (6.) It is improper to say, "*The simple word becomes* [the] *comparative by adding r or er*; and *the superlative by adding st or est.*" The thought is wrong; and nearly all the words are misapplied; as, *simple* for *primitive, adding* for *assuming*, &c. (7.) Nor is it very wise to say, "the adverbs *more* and *most*, placed before the adjective, *have the same effect*:" because it ought to be known, that the effect of the one is very different from that of the other! "*The same effect,*" cannot here be taken for any effect previously described; unless we will have it to be, that these words, *more* and *most,* "become comparative by adding *r* or *er*; and the superlative by adding *st* or *est,* to the end of them:" all of which is grossly absurd. (8.) The repetition of the word *degree,* in saying, "The superlative *degree* increases or lessens the positive to the highest or lowest *degree,*" is a disagreeable tautology. Besides, unless it involves the additional error of presenting the same word in different senses, it makes one degree swell or diminish an other *to itself*; whereas, in the very next sentence, this singular agency is forgotten, and a second equally strange takes its place: "The positive *becomes* the superlative by adding *st* or *est,* to the end of it;" i. e., to the end of *itself.* Nothing can be more ungrammatical, than is much of the language by which grammar itself is now professedly taught!

OBS. 5.—It has been almost universally assumed by grammarians, that the positive degree is *the only standard* to which the other degrees can refer; though many seem to think, that the superlative always implies or includes the comparative, and is consequently inapplicable when only two things are spoken of. Neither of these positions is involved in any of the definitions which I have given above. The reader may think what he will about these points, after observing the several ways in which each form may be used. In the phrases, "*greater* than Solomon,"—"*more* than a bushel,"—"*later* than one o'clock," it is not immediately obvious that the positives *great, much,* and *late,* are the real terms of contrast. And how is it in the Latin phrases, "*Dulcior melle,* sweeter than honey,"—"*Præstantior auro,* better than gold?" These authors will resolve all such phrases thus: "*greater,* than Solomon *was great,*"—"*more,* than a bushel *is much,*" &c. As the conjunction *than* never governs the objective case, it seems necessary to suppose an ellipsis of some verb after the noun which follows it as above; and possibly the foregoing solution, uncouth as it seems, may, for the English idiom, be the true one: as, "My Father is *greater than I.*"—*John,* xiv, 28. That is, "My Father is greater *than I am*;"—or, perhaps, "than I am *great*." But if it appear that *some* degree of the same quality must always be contrasted with the comparative, there is still room to question whether this degree must always be that which we call the positive. Cicero, in exile, wrote to his wife: "Ego autem hoc *miserior* sum, quam tu, quæ es *miserrima*, quod ipsa calamitas communis est utriusque nostrùm, sed culpa mea propria est."—*Epist. ad Fam.*, xiv, 3. "But in this I am *more wretched*, than thou, who art *most wretched*, that the calamity itself is common to us both, but the fault is all my own."

OBS. 6.—In my Institutes and First Lines of English Grammar, I used the following brief definitions: "The *comparative degree* is that which exceeds the positive; as, *harder, softer, better*." "The *superlative degree* is that which is not exceeded; as, *hardest, softest, best*." And it is rather for the sake of suggesting to the learner the peculiar *application* of each of these degrees, than from any decided dissatisfaction with these expressions, that I now present others. The first, however, proceeds upon the common supposition, that the comparative degree of a quality, ascribed to any object, must needs be contrasted with the positive in some other, or with the positive in the same at an other time. This idea may be plausibly maintained, though it is certain that the positive term referred to, is seldom, if ever, allowed to appear. Besides, the comparative or the superlative *may* appear, and in such a manner as to be, or seem to be, in the point of contrast. Thus: "Objects near our view are apt to be thought *greater than those of a larger size*, that are more remote."—*Locke's Essay*, p. 186. Upon the principle above, the explanation here must be, that the meaning is —"*greater* than those of a larger size *are thought great*." "The *poor* man that loveth Christ, is *richer than the richest man* in the world, that hates him."—*Bunyan's Pilgrim's Progress*, p. 86. This must be "*richer* than the richest man *is rich*." The riches contemplated here, are of different sorts; and the comparative or the superlative of one sort, may be exceeded by either of these degrees of an other sort, though the same epithet be used for both. So in the following instances: "He that is *higher than the highest* regardeth; and there be *higher than they*."—*Eccl.*, v, 8. That is, "He that is higher than the highest *earthly dignitaries*, regardeth; and there are higher *authorities* than *these*." "*Fairer* than aught imagined else *fairest*."—*Pollok*. "*Sadder than saddest* night."—*Byron*. It is evident that the superlative degree is not, in general, that which *cannot be* exceeded, but that which, in the actual state of the things included, "*is* not exceeded." Again, as soon as any given comparative or superlative is, by a further elevation or intension of the quality, surpassed and exceeded, that particular degree, whatever it was, becomes merely positive; for the positive degree of a quality, though it commonly includes the very lowest measure, and is understood to exceed nothing, may at any time *equal* the very highest. There is no paradox in all this, which is not also in the following simple examples: "*Easier*, indeed, I was, but far from *easy*."—*Cowper's Life*, p. 50.

"Who canst the *wisest wiser* make,
And babes *as wise* as they."—*Cowper's Poems*.

OBS. 7.—The relative nature of these degrees deserves to be further illustrated. (1.) It is plain, that the greatest degree of a quality in one thing, may be less than the least in an other; and, consequently, that the least degree in one thing, may be greater than the greatest in an other. Thus, the *heaviest* wood is *less heavy* than the *lightest* of the metals; and the *least valuable* of the metals is perhaps of *more value* than the *choicest* wood. (2.) The comparative degree may increase upon itself, and be repeated to show the gradation. Thus, a man may ascend into the air with a balloon, and rise *higher*, and *higher*, and *higher*, and *higher*, till he is out of sight. This is no uncommon form of expression, and the intension is from comparative to comparative. (3.) If a ladder be set up for use, one of its rounds will be *the highest*, and one other will be *the lowest*, or *least high*. And as that which is *highest,* is *higher* than all the rest, so every one will be *higher* than all below it. *The higher rounds,* if spoken of generally, and without definite contrast, will be those in the upper half; *the lower rounds,* referred to in like manner, will be those in the lower half, or those not far from the ground. *The highest rounds,* or *the lowest,* if we indulge such latitude of speech, will be those near the top or the bottom; there being, absolutely, or in *strictness* of language, but *one* of each. (4.) If *the highest* round be removed, or left uncounted, the next becomes the *highest,* though not *so high* as the former. For every one is *the highest* of the number which it completes. All admit this, till we come to *three.* And, as the third is *the highest of the three,* I see not why the second is not properly *the highest of the two.* Yet nearly all our grammarians condemn this phrase, and prefer "*the higher of the two.*" But can they give a *reason* for their preference? That the comparative degree is implied between the positive and the superlative, so that there must needs be three terms before the latter is applicable, is a doctrine which I deny. And if the second is *the higher of the two,* because it is *higher than the first*; is it not also *the highest of the two,* because it *completes the number?* (5.) It is to be observed, too, that as our ordinal numeral *first,* denoting the one which begins a series, and having reference of course to more, is an adjective of the superlative degree, equivalent to *foremost,* of which it is perhaps a contraction; so *last* likewise, though no numeral, is a superlative also. (6.) These, like other superlatives, admit of a looser application, and may possibly include more than one thing at the beginning or at the end of a series: as, "*The last years* of man are often helpless, like *the first.*" (7.) With undoubted propriety, we may speak of *the first two, the last two, the first three, the last three,* &c.; but to say, *the two first, the two last,* &c., with this meaning, is obviously and needlessly inaccurate. "*The two first men* in the nation," may, I admit, be good English; but it can properly be meant only of *the two most eminent.* In specifying any part of a *series,* we ought rather to place the cardinal number after the ordinal. (8.) Many of the foregoing positions apply generally, to almost all adjectives that are susceptible of comparison. Thus, it is a common saying, "Take *the best first*, and *all* will be *best*." That is, remove that degree which is now superlative, and the epithet will descend to an other, "*the next best*."

OBS. 8.—It is a common assumption, maintained by almost all our grammarians, that the degrees which add to the adjective the terminations *er* and *est*, as well as those which are expressed by *more* and *most*, indicate an *increase*, or heightening, of the quality expressed by the positive. If such must needs be their import, it is certainly very improper, to apply them, as many do, to what can be only an approximation to the positive. Thus Dr. Blair: "Nothing that belongs to human nature, is *more universal* than the relish of beauty of one kind or other."—*Lectures*, p. 16. "In architecture, the Grecian models were long esteemed *the most perfect*."—*Ib.*, p. 20. Again: In his reprehension of Capernaum, the Saviour said, "It shall be *more tolerable* for the land of Sodom, in the day of judgement, than for thee."—*Matt.*, xi, 24. Now, although [Greek: anektoteron], *more tolerable*, is in itself a good comparative, who would dare infer from this text, that in the day of judgement Capernaum shall fare *tolerably*, and Sodom, *still better*? There is much reason to think, that the essential nature of these grammatical degrees has not been well understood by those who have heretofore pretended to explain them. If we except those few approximations to sensible qualities, which are signified by such words as *whitish, greenish, &c.*, there will be found no actual measure, or inherent degree of any quality, to which the simple form of the adjective is not applicable; or which, by the help of intensive adverbs of a positive character, it may not be made to express; and that, too, without becoming either comparative or superlative, in the technical sense of those terms. Thus *very white, exceedingly white, perfectly white*, are terms quite as significant as *whiter* and *whitest*, if not more so. Some grammarians, observing this, and knowing that the Romans often used their superlative in a sense merely intensive, as *altissimus* for *very high*, have needlessly divided our English superlative into two, "*the definite*, and the *indefinite*;" giving the latter name to that degree which we mark by the adverb *very*, and the former to that which alone is properly called the superlative. Churchill does this: while, (as we have seen above,) in naming the degrees, he pretends to prefer "what has been established by long custom."—*New Gram.*, p. 231. By a strange oversight also, he failed to notice, that this doctrine interferes with his scheme of *five* degrees, and would clearly furnish him with *six*: to which if he had chosen to add the "*imperfect degree*" of Dr. Webster, (as *whitish, greenish, &c.*,) which is recognized by Johnson, Murray, and others, he might have had *seven*. But I hope my readers will by-and-by believe there is *no need* of more than *three*.

OBS. 9.—The true nature of the Comparative degree is this: it denotes either some *excess* or some *relative deficiency* of the quality, when one thing or party is compared with an other, in respect to what is in both: as, "Because the foolishness of God is *wiser* than men; and the weakness of God is *stronger* than men."—*1 Cor.*, i, 25. "Few languages are, in fact, *more copious* than the English."—*Blair's Rhet.*, p. 87. "Our style is *less compact* than that of the ancients."—*Ib.*, p. 88. "They are counted to him *less* than nothing and vanity."—*Isaiah*, xl, 17. As the comparatives in a long *series* are necessarily many, and some of them *higher* than others, it may be asked, "How can the comparative degree, in this case, be merely 'that which exceeds the positive?'" Or, as our common grammarians prompt me here to say, "May not the comparative degree increase or lessen *the comparative*, in signification?" The latter form of the question they may answer for themselves; remembering that the comparative *may advance from the comparative*, step by step, from the second article in the series to the utmost. Thus, three is a higher or greater number than two; but four is higher than three; five, than four; and so on, *ad infinitum*. My own form of the question I answer thus: "The *highest* of the *higher* is not *higher* than the rest are *higher*, but simply *higher* than they are *high*."

OBS. 10.—The true nature of the Superlative degree is this: it denotes, in a quality, *some extreme* or *unsurpassed extent*. It may be used either absolutely, as being without bounds; or relatively, as being confined within any limits we choose to give it. It is equally applicable to that which is naturally unsurpassable, and to that which stands within the narrowest limits of comparison. The *heaviest* of *three feathers* would scarcely be thought a *heavy* thing, and yet the expression is proper; because the weight, whatever it is, is relatively *the greatest*. The *youngest* of three persons, may not be *very young*; nor need we suppose the *oldest* in a whole college to have arrived at *the greatest conceivable age*. What then shall be thought of the explanations which our grammarians have given of this degree of comparison? That of Murray I have already criticised. It is ascribed to him, not upon the supposition that he invented it; but because common sense continues to give place to the authority of his name in support of it. Comly, Russell, Alger, Ingersoll, Greenleaf, Fisk, Merchant, Kirkham, T. Smith, R. C. Smith, Hall, Hiley, and many others, have copied it into their grammars, as being better than any definition they could devise. Murray himself unquestionably took it from some obscure pedagogue among the old grammarians. Buchanan, who long preceded him, has nearly the same words: "The Superlative increases or diminishes the Positive in Signification, to the highest or [the] lowest Degree of all."—*English Syntax*, p. 28. If this is to be taken for a grammatical definition, what definition shall grammar itself bear?

OBS. 11.—Let us see whether our later authors have done better. "The *superlative* expresses a quality in the greatest or [the] least *possible* degree; as, *wisest, coldest, least wise*."—*Webster's Old Gram.*, p. 13. In his later speculations, this author conceives that the termination *ish* forms the *first* degree of comparison; as, "Imperfect, *dankish*," Pos. *dank*, Comp. *danker*, Superl. *dankest.* "There are therefore *four* degrees of comparison."—*Webster's Philosophical Gram.* p. 65. "The *fourth* denotes the utmost or [the] least degree of a quality; as, *bravest, wisest, poorest, smallest.* This is called the *superlative* degree."—*Ib.*; also his *Improved Gram.*, 1831, p. 47. "This degree is called the Superlative degree, from its raising the amount of the quality above that of all others."—*Webber's Gram.*, 1832, p. 26. It is not easy to quote, from any source, a worse sentence than this; if, indeed, so strange a jumble of words can be called a sentence. "*From its raising the amount,*" is in itself a vicious and untranslatable phrase, here put for "*because it raises the amount;*" and who can conceive of the superlative degree, as "*raising the amount of the quality* above that of *all other qualities*?" Or, if it be supposed to mean, "above the amount of all other *degrees,*" what is this amount? Is it that of one and one, the *positive* and the *comparative* added numerically? or is it the sum of all the quantities which these may indicate? Perhaps the author meant, "above the amount of all other *amounts.*" If none of these absurdities is here taught, nothing is taught, and the words are nonsense. Again: "The *superlative degree* increases or diminishes the positive to the highest or [the] lowest degree *of which it is susceptible.*"—*Bucke's Classical Gram.*, p. 49. "The superlative degree is generally formed by adding *st* or *est* to the positive; and denotes *the greatest excess.*"—*Nutting's Gram.*, p. 33. "The Superlative increases or diminishes the Signification of the Positive or Adjective, to a *very high* or a *very low* Degree."—*British Gram.*, p. 97. What *excess* of skill, or what *very high degree* of acuteness, have the *brightest* and *best* of these grammarians exhibited? There must be some, if their definitions are *true*.

OBS. 12.—The common assertion of the grammarians, that the superlative degree is not applicable to two *objects,*[177] is not only unsupported by any reason in the nature of things, but it is contradicted in practice by almost every man who affirms it. Thus Maunder: "When only two persons or things are spoken of comparatively, to use the superlative is improper: as, 'Deborah, my dear, give those two boys a lump of sugar each; and let Dick's be the largest, because he spoke first.' This," says the critic, "should have been 'larger.'"—*Maunder's Gram.*, p. 4. It is true, the comparative *might* here have been used; but the superlative is clearer, and more agreeable to custom. And how can "*largest*" be wrong, if "*first*" is right? "Let Dick's be the *larger*, because he spoke *sooner*," borders too much upon a different idea, that of *proportion*; as when we say, "*The sooner the better*,"—"*The more the merrier*." So Blair: "When only two things are compared, the comparative degree should be used, and not the superlative."—*Practical Gram.*, p. 81. "A Trochee has the *first* syllable accented, and the *last* unaccented."—*Ib.*, p. 118. "An Iambus has the first syllable unaccented, and the *last* accented."—*Ibid.* These two examples are found also in *Jamieson's Rhetoric*, p. 305; *Murray's Gram.*, p. 253; *Kirkham's*, 219; *Bullions's*, 169; *Guy's*, 120; *Merchant's*, 166. So Hiley: "When *two* persons or things are compared, the *comparative* degree must be employed. When *three or more* persons or things are compared, the *superlative* must be used."—*Treatise on English Gram.*, p. 78. Contradiction in practice: "Thomas is *wiser* than his brothers."—*Ib.*, p. 79. Are not "*three or more persons*" here compared by "the comparative" *wiser*? "In an *Iambus* the *first* syllable is unaccented."—*Ib.*, p. 123. An iambus has but *two* syllables; and this author expressly teaches that "*first*" is "superlative."—*Ib.*, p. 21. So Sanborn: "The *positive* degree denotes the *simple* form of an adjective *without* any variation of meaning. The *comparative* degree increases or lessens the meaning *of the positive*, and denotes a comparison *between two* persons or things. The *superlative* degree increases or lessens the positive *to the greatest extent*, and denotes a comparison *between more than two* persons or things."—*Analytical Gram.*, p. 30 and p. 86. These pretended definitions of the degrees of comparison embrace not only the absurdities which I have already censured in those of our common grammars, but several new ones peculiar to this author. Of the inconsistency of his doctrine and practice, take the following examples: "Which of two bodies, that move with the same velocity, will exercise the *greatest* power?"—*Ib.*, p. 93; and again, p. 203, "'I was offered a *dollar*;'—'A *dollar* was offered (to) *me*.' The *first* form should always be avoided."—*Ib.*, p. 127. "Nouns in apposition generally annex the sign of the possessive case to the *last*; as, 'For David my *servant's* sake.'—'John the *Baptist's* head.' *Bible*."—*Ib.*, p. 197.

OBS. 13.—So Murray: "We commonly say, 'This is the *weaker of the two*;' or, 'The *weakest* of the two;'[178] but the former is the regular mode of expression, because there are *only two* things compared."—*Octavo Gram.*, i, 167. What then of the following example: "Which of *those two persons* has *most* distinguished himself?"—*Ib., Key*, ii, 187. Again, in treating of the adjectives *this* and *that*, the same hand writes thus: "*This* refers to the *nearest* person or thing, and *that* to the *most distant*: as, 'This man is *more intelligent* than *that*.' *This* indicates the *latter*, or *last* mentioned; *that*, the *former*, or *first* mentioned: as, 'Both wealth and poverty are temptations; *that* tends to excite pride, *this*, discontent.'"—*Murray's Gram.*, i, 56. In the former part of this example, the superlative is twice applied where only two things are spoken of; and, in the latter, it is twice made equivalent to the comparative, with a like reference. The following example shows the same equivalence: "*This* refers to the *last* mentioned or *nearer* thing, *that* to the *first* mentioned or *more* distant thing."—*Webber's Gram.*, p. 31. So Churchill: "The superlative should not be used, when only two persons or things are compared."—*New Gram.*, p. 80. "In the *first* of these two sentences."—*Ib.*, p. 162; *Lowth*, p. 120. According to the rule, it should have been, "In the *former* of these two sentences;" but this would be here ambiguous, because *former* might mean *maker*. "When our sentence consists of two members, the *longest* should, generally, be the concluding one."—*Blair's Rhet.*, p. 117: and *Jamieson's*, p. 99. "The *shortest* member being placed *first,* we carry it *more readily* in our memory as we proceed to the second."—*Ib.,* & *Ib.* "Pray consider us, in this respect, as the *weakest* sex."—*Spect.,* No. 533. In this last sentence, the comparative, *weaker,* would perhaps have been better; because, not an absolute, but merely a comparative weakness is meant. So Latham and Child: "It is better, in speaking of only two objects, to use the comparative degree rather than the superlative, even, where we use the article *the. This is the better of the two,* is preferable to *this is the best of the two.*"—*Elementary Gram.,* p. 155. Such is their rule; but very soon they forget it, and write thus: "In this case the relative refers to the *last* of the two."—*Ib.,* p. 163.

OBS. 14.—Hyperboles are very commonly expressed by comparatives or superlatives; as, "My *little finger* shall be *thicker* than my *father's loins.*"— *1 Kings,* xii, 10. "Unto me, who am *less than the least* of all saints, is this grace given."—*Ephesians,* iii, 8. Sometimes, in thus heightening or lowering the object of his conception, the writer falls into a catachresis, solecism, or abuse of the grammatical degrees; as, "Mustard-seed—which is *less than all the seeds* that be in the earth."—*Mark,* iv, 31. This expression is objectionable, because mustard-seed is a seed, and cannot be less than itself; though that which is here spoken of, may perhaps have been "*the least of all seeds*:" and it is the same Greek phrase, that is thus rendered in Matt, xiii, 32. Murray has inserted in his Exercises, among "unintelligible and inconsistent words and phrases," the following example from Milton:

"And, in the lowest deep, a lower deep
Still threat'ning to devour me, opens wide."—*Exercises,* p. 122.

For this supposed inconsistency, ho proposes in his Key the following amendment:

"And, in the *lower* deep, *another* deep
Still threat'ning to devour me, opens wide."—*Key,* p. 254.

But, in an other part of his book, he copies from Dr. Blair the same passage, with commendation: saying, "The following sentiments of *Satan in Milton*, as strongly as they are described, *contain nothing* but what is *natural and proper*:

'Me miserable! which way shall I fly
Infinite wrath, and infinite despair?
Which way I fly is Hell; myself am Hell;
And in the lowest *depth*, a lower deep,
Still threat'ning to devour me, opens wide,
To which the Hell I suffer seems a Heaven.' *P. Lost*, B. iv, l. 73."
Blair's Lectures, p. 153; *Murray's Grammar*, p. 352.

OBS. 15.—Milton's word, in the fourth line above, is *deep*, and not *depth*, as these authors here give it: nor was it very polite in them, to use a phraseology which comes so near to saying, the devil was in the poet. Alas for grammar! accuracy in its teachers has become the most rare of all qualifications. As for Murray's correction above, I see not how it can please any one who chooses to think Hell a place of great depth. A descent into his "*lower* deep" and "*other* deep," might be a plunge less horrible than two or three successive slides in one of our western caverns! But Milton supposes the arch-fiend might descend to the lowest *imaginable* depth of Hell, and there be liable to a still further fall of more tremendous extent. Fall whither? Into the horrid and inconceivable profundity of the *bottomless pit*! What signifies it, to object to his language as "*unintelligible*" if it conveys his idea better than any other could? In no human conception of what is infinite, can there be any real exaggeration. To amplify beyond the truth, is here impossible. Nor is there any superlation which can fix a limit to the idea of more and more in infinitude. Whatever literal absurdity there may be in it, the duplication seems greatly to augment what was even our greatest conception of the thing. Homer, with a like figure, though expressed in the positive degree, makes Jupiter threaten any rebel god, that he shall be thrown down from Olympus, to suffer the burning pains of the Tartarean gulf; not in the centre, but,

"As *deep* beneath th' infernal centre hurl'd,
As from that centre to th' ethereal world."
　　—*Pope's Iliad*, B. viii, l. 19.

REGULAR COMPARISON.

Adjectives are regularly compared, when the comparative degree is expressed by adding *er*, and the superlative, by adding *est* to them: as, Pos., *great*, Comp., *greater*, Superl., *greatest*; Pos., *mild*, Comp., *milder*, Superl., *mildest*.

In the variation of adjectives, final consonants are doubled, final *e* is omitted, and final *y* is changed to *i*, agreeably to the rules for spelling: as, *hot, hotter, hottest; wide, wider, widest; happy, happier, happiest*.

The regular method of comparison belongs almost exclusively to monosyllables, with dissyllables ending in *w* or *y*, and such others as receive it and still have but one syllable after the accent: as, *fierce, fiercer, fiercest; narrow, narrower, narrowest; gloomy, gloomier, gloomiest; serene, serener, serenest; noble, nobler, noblest; gentle, gentler, gentlest*.

COMPARISON BY ADVERBS.

The two degrees of superiority may also be expressed with precisely the same import as above, by prefixing to the adjective the adverbs *more* and *most*: as, *wise, more wise, most wise; famous, more famous, most famous; amiable, more amiable, most amiable*.

The degrees of inferiority are expressed, in like manner, by the adverbs *less* and *least*: as, *wise, less wise, least wise; famous, less famous, least famous; amiable, less amiable, least amiable.* The regular method of comparison has, properly speaking, no degrees of this kind.

Nearly all adjectives that admit of different degrees, may be compared by means of the adverbs; but, for short words, the regular method is generally preferable: as, *quick, quicker, quickest*; rather than, *quick, more quick, most quick.*

OBSERVATIONS.

OBS. 1.—The genius of our language is particularly averse to the lengthening of long words by additional syllables; and, in the comparison of adjectives, *er* and *est* always add a syllable to the word, except it end in *le* after a mute. Thus, *free, freer, freest*, increases syllabically; but *ample, ampler, amplest,* does not. Whether any particular adjective admits of comparison or not, is a matter of reasoning from the sense of the term; by which method it shall be compared, is in some degree a matter of taste; though custom has decided that long words shall not be inflected, and for the shorter, there is generally an obvious bias in favour of one form rather than the other. Dr. Johnson says, "The comparison of adjectives is very uncertain; and being much regulated by commodiousness of utterance, or agreeableness of sound, is not easily reduced to rules. Monosyllables are commonly compared. Polysyllables, or words of more than two syllables, are seldom compared otherwise than by *more* and *most*. Dissyllables are seldom compared if they terminate in *full, less, ing, ous, ed, id, at, ent, ain, or ive.*"—*Gram. of the English Tongue*, p. 6. "When the positive contains but one syllable, the degrees are usually formed by adding *er* or *est*. When the positive contains two syllables, it is matter of taste which method you shall use in forming the degrees. The ear is, in this case, the best guide. But, when the positive contains more than two syllables, the degrees must be formed by the use of *more* and *most*. We may say, *tenderer* and *tenderest, pleasanter* and *pleasantest, prettier* and *prettiest*; but who could endure *delicater* and *delicatest*?"—*Cobbett's E. Gram.*, p. 81. *Quiet, bitter, clever, sober,* and perhaps some others like them, are still regularly compared; but such words as *secretest, famousest, virtuousest, powerfullest,* which were used by Milton, have gone out of fashion. The following, though not very commonly used, are perhaps allowable. "Yet these are the two *commonest* occupations of mankind."—*Philological Museum*, i, 431. "Their *pleasantest* walks throughout life must be guarded by armed men."—*Ib.*, i, 437. "Franklin possessed the rare talent of drawing useful lessons from the *commonest* occurrences."—*Murray's Sequel*, p. 323. "Unbidden guests are often *welcomest* when they are gone."—SHAK.: *in Joh. Dict.*

　"There was a lad, th' *unluckiest* of his crew,
　Was still contriving something bad, but new."—KING: *ib.*

OBS. 2.—I make a distinction between the regular comparison by *er* and *est*, and the comparison by adverbs; because, in a grammatical point of view, these two methods are totally different: the meaning, though the same, being expressed in the one case, by an inflection of the adjective; and in the other, by a phrase consisting of two different parts of speech. If the placing of an adverb before an adjective is to be called a grammatical modification or variation of the latter word, we shall have many other degrees than those which are enumerated above. The words may with much more propriety be parsed separately, the degree being ascribed to the adverb—or, if you please, to both words, for both are varied in sense by the inflection of the former. The degrees in which qualities may exist in nature, are infinitely various; but the only degrees with which the grammarian is concerned, are those which our variation of the adjective or adverb enables us to express—including, as of course we must, the state or sense of the primitive word, as one. The reasoning which would make the positive degree to be no degree, would also make the nominative case, or the *casus rectus* of the Latins, to be no case.

OBS. 3.—Whenever the adjective itself denotes these degrees, and is duly varied in form to express them, they properly belong to it; as, *worthy, worthier, worthiest.* (Though no apology can be made for the frequent error of confounding the *degree of a quality,* with the *verbal sign* which expresses it.) If an adverb is employed for this purpose, that also is compared, and the two degrees thus formed or expressed, are properly its own; as, worthy, *more* worthy, *most* worthy. But these same degrees may be yet otherwise expressed; as, worthy, *in a higher degree* worthy, *in the highest degree* worthy. Here also the adjective *worthy* is virtually compared, as before; but only the adjective *high* is grammatically modified. Again, we may form three degrees with several adverbs to each, thus: Pos., *very truly* worthy; Comp., *much more truly* worthy; Sup., *much the most truly* worthy. There are also other adverbs, which, though not varied in themselves like *much, more, most,* may nevertheless have nearly the same effect upon the adjective; as, worthy, *comparatively* worthy, *superlatively* worthy. I make these remarks, because many grammarians have erroneously parsed the adverbs *more* and *most, less* and *least,* as parts of the adjective.

OBS. 4.—Harris, in his Hermes, or Philosophical Inquiry concerning Universal Grammar, has very unceremoniously pronounced the doctrine of three degrees of comparison, to be *absurd*; and the author of the British Grammar, as he emotes the whole passage without offering any defence of that doctrine, seems to second the allegation. "Mr. Harris observes, that, 'There cannot well be more than two degrees; one to denote simple excess, and one to denote superlative. Were we indeed to introduce more degrees, we ought perhaps to introduce infinite, which is absurd. For why stop at a limited number, when in all subjects, susceptible of intension, the intermediate excesses are in a manner infinite? There are infinite degrees of *more white* between the first simple *white* and the superlative *whitest*; the same may be said of *more great, more strong, more minute,* &c. The doctrine of grammarians about *three* such degrees, which they call the Positive, the Comparative, and the Superlative, must needs be absurd; both because in their Positive there is no comparison at all, and because their Superlative is a Comparative as much as their Comparative itself.' *Hermes,* p. 197."—*Brit. Gram.,* p. 98. This objection is rashly urged. No comparison can be imagined without bringing together as many as two terms, and if the positive is one of these, it is a degree of comparison; though neither this nor the superlative is, for that reason, "*a Comparative.*" Why we stop at three degrees, I have already shown: we have three *forms,* and only three.

OBS. 5.—"The termination *ish* may be accounted in some sort a degree of comparison, by which the signification is diminished below the positive, as *black, blackish,* or tending to blackness; *salt, saltish,* or having a little taste of salt:[179] they therefore admit of no comparison. This termination is seldom added but to words expressing sensible qualities, nor often to words of above one syllable, and is scarcely used in the solemn or sublime style."—*Dr. Johnson's Gram.* "The *first* [degree] denotes a slight degree of the quality, and is expressed by the termination *ish*; as, *reddish, brownish, yellowish.* This may be denominated the *imperfect* degree of the attribute."—*Dr. Webster's Improved Gram.,* p. 47. I doubt the correctness of the view taken above by Johnson, and dissent entirely from Webster, about his "*first degree* of comparison." Of adjectives in *ish* we have perhaps a hundred; but nine out of ten of them are derived clearly from *nouns,* as, *boyish, girlish*; and who can prove that *blackish, saltish, reddish, brownish,* and *yellowish,* are not also from the *nouns, black, salt, red, brown,* and *yellow*? or that "a *more reddish* tinge,"—"a *more saltish* taste," are not correct phrases? There is, I am persuaded, no good reason for noticing this termination as constituting a degree of comparison. All "double comparisons" are said to be ungrammatical; but, if *ish* forms a degree, it is such a degree as may be compared again: as,

"And seem *more learnedish* than those
That at a greater charge compose."—*Butler.*

OBS. 6.—Among the degrees of comparison, some have enumerated that of *equality*; as when we say, "It is *as sweet as* honey." Here is indeed a comparison, but it is altogether in the *positive* degree, and needs no other name. This again refutes Harris; who says, that in the positive there is no comparison at all. But further: it is plain, that in this degree there may be comparisons of *inequality* also; as, "Molasses is *not so sweet* as honey."—"Civility is *not so slight* a matter as it is commonly thought."—*Art of Thinking*, p. 92. Nay, such comparisons may equal any superlative. Thus it is said, I think, in the Life of Robert Hall: "Probably no human being ever before suffered *so much* bodily pain." What a preëminence is here! and yet the form of the adjective is only that of the positive degree. "Nothing *so uncertain* as general reputation."—*Art of Thinking*, p. 50. "Nothing *so nauseous* as undistinguishing civility."—*Ib.*, p. 88. These, likewise, would be strong expressions, if they were correct English. But, to my apprehension, every such comparison of equality involves a solecism, when, as it here happens, the former term includes the latter. The word *nothing* is a general negative, and *reputation* is a particular affirmative. The comparison of equality between them, is therefore certainly improper: because *nothing* cannot be equal to *something*; and, reputation being something, and of course equal to itself, the proposition is evidently untrue. It ought to be, "Nothing *is more uncertain than* general reputation." This is the same as to say, "General reputation is *as uncertain as any thing* that can be named." Or else the former term should exempt the latter; as. "*Nothing else*"—or, "No *other* thing, is *so uncertain* as" *this popular honour, public esteem,* or "*general reputation.*" And so of all similar examples.

OBS. 7.—In all comparisons, care must be taken to adapt the terms to the degree which is expressed by the adjective or adverb. The superlative degree requires that the object to which it relates, be one of those with which it is compared; as, "*Eve* was *the fairest* of women." The comparative degree, on the contrary, requires that the object spoken of be not included among those with which it is compared; as, "*Eve* was *fairer* than any of *her daughters.*" To take the inclusive term here, and say, "*Eve* was *fairer* than any *woman,*" would be no less absurd, than Milton's assertion, that "Eve was *the fairest* of *her daughters:*" the former supposes that she was *not a woman*; the latter, that she was *one of her own daughters*. But Milton's solecism is double; he makes Adam *one of his own sons*:—

"Adam the goodliest man of men since born
His sons, the fairest of her daughters Eve."—*P. Lost*, B. iv, l. 324.

OBS. 8.—"Such adjectives," says Churchill, "as have in themselves a superlative signification, or express qualities not susceptible of degrees, do not properly admit either the comparative or [the] superlative form. Under this rule may be included *all adjectives with a negative prefix.*"—*New Gram.*, p. 80. Again: "As *immediate* signifies instant, present with regard to time, Prior should not have written '*more* immediate.' *Dr. Johnson.*"—*Ib.*, p. 233. "Hooker has *unaptest*; Locke, *more uncorrupted*; Holder, *more undeceivable*: for these the proper expressions would have been the opposite signs without the negation: *least apt, less corrupted, less deceivable*. Watts speaks of 'a *most unpassable* barrier.' If he had simply said 'an unpassable barrier,' we should have understood it at once in the strongest sense, as a barrier impossible to be surmounted: but, by attempting to express something more, he gives an idea of something less; we perceive, that his *unpassable* means *difficult to pass*. This is the mischief of the propensity to exaggeration; which, striving after strength, sinks into weakness."—*Ib.*, p. 234.

OBS. 9.—The foregoing remarks from Churchill appear *in general* to have been dictated by good sense; but, if his own practice is right, there must be some exceptions to his rule respecting the comparison of adjectives with a negative prefix; for, in the phrase "*less imprudent,*" which, according to a passage quoted before, he will have to be different from "*more prudent,*" he himself furnishes an example of such comparison. In fact, very many words of that class are compared by good writers: as, "Nothing is *more unnecessary.*"—*Lowth's Gram., Pref.*, p. v. "What is yet *more unaccountable.*"—ROGERS: *in Joh. Dict.* "It is hard to determine which is *most uneligible.*"—*Id., ib.* "Where it appears the *most unbecoming* and *unnatural.*"—ADDISON: *ib.* "Men of the best sense and of the *most unblemished* lives."—*Id., ib.* "March and September are the *most unsettled* and *unequable* of seasons."—BENTLEY: *ib.* "Barcelona was taken by a *most unexpected* accident."—SWIFT: *ib.* "The *most barren* and *unpleasant.*"—WOODWARD: *ib.* "O good, but *most unwise* patricians!"—SHAK.: *ib.* "*More unconstant* than the wind."—*Id., ib.* "We may say *more* or *less imperfect.*"—*Murray's Gram.*, p. 168. "Some of those [passions] which act with the *most irresistible* energy upon the hearts of mankind, are altogether omitted in the catalogue of Aristotle."—*Adams's Rhet.*, i, 380. "The wrong of him who presumes to talk of owning me, is *too unmeasured* to be softened by kindness."—*Channing, on Emancipation*, p. 52. "Which, we are sensible, are *more inconclusive* than the rest."—*Blair's Rhet.*, p. 319.

"Ere yet the salt of *most unrighteous* tears
Had left the flushing in her galled eyes."—*Shak.*

OBS. 10.—Comparison must not be considered a general property of adjectives. It belongs chiefly to the class which I call common adjectives, and is by no means applicable to all of these. *Common adjectives,* or epithets denoting quality, are perhaps more numerous than all the other classes put together. Many of these, and a few that are pronominal, may be varied by comparison; and some *participial* adjectives may be compared by means of the adverbs. But adjectives formed from *proper names*, all the numerals, and most of the compounds, are in no way susceptible of comparison. All nouns used adjectively, as an *iron* bar, an *evening* school, a *mahogany* chair, a *South-Sea* dream, are also incapable of comparison. In the title of "His *Most Christian* Majesty," the superlative adverb is applied to a *proper adjective*; but who will pretend that we ought to understand by it "*the highest degree*" of Christian attainment? It might seem uncourtly to suggest that this is "an abuse of the king's English," I shall therefore say no such thing. Pope compares the word Christian, in the following couplet:—

"Go, purified by flames ascend the sky,
My better and *more Christian* progeny."—*Dunciad*, B. i, l. 227.

IRREGULAR COMPARISON.

The following adjectives are compared irregularly: *good, better, best; bad, evil*, or *ill, worse, worst; little, less, least; much, more, most; many, more, most.*

OBSERVATIONS.

OBS. 1.—In *English*, and also in *Latin*, most adjectives that denote *place* or *situation*, not only form the superlative irregularly, but are also either defective or redundant in comparison. Thus:

I. The following nine have more than one superlative: *far, farther, farthest, farmost*, or *farthermost; near, nearer, nearest* or *next; fore, former, foremost* or *first; hind, hinder, hindmost* or *hindermost; in, inner, inmost* or *innermost; out, outer*, or *utter, outmost* or *utmost, outermost* or *uttermost;*

up, upper, upmost or *uppermost; low, lower, lowest* or *lowermost; late, later* or *latter, latest* or *last.*

II. The following five want the positive: [*aft*, adv.,] *after, aftmost* or *aftermost*; [*forth*, adv., formerly *furth*,[180]] *further, furthest* or *furthermost; hither, hithermost; nether, nethermost; under, undermost.*

III. The following want the comparative: *front, frontmost; rear, rearmost; head, headmost; end, endmost; top, topmost; bottom, bottommost; mid* or *middle, midst,[181] midmost* or *middlemost; north, northmost; south, southmost; east, eastmost; west, westmost; northern, northernmost; southern, southernmost; eastern, easternmost; western, westernmost.*

OBS. 2.—Many of these irregular words are not always used as adjectives, but oftener as nouns, adverbs, or prepositions. The sense in which they are employed, will show to what class they belong. The terms *fore* and *hind, front* and *rear, right* and *left, in* and *out, high* and *low, top* and *bottom, up* and *down, upper* and *under, mid* and *after*, all but the last pair, are in direct contrast with each other. Many of them are often joined in composition with other words; and some, when used as adjectives of place, are rarely separated from their nouns: as, _in_land, _out_house, *mid*-sea, *after*-ages. Practice is here so capricious, I find it difficult to determine whether the compounding of these terms is proper or not. It is a case about which he that inquires most, may perhaps be most in doubt. If the joining of the words prevents the possibility of mistaking the adjective for a preposition, it prevents also the separate classification of the adjective and the noun, and thus in some sense destroys the former by making the whole a noun. Dr. Webster writes thus: "FRONTROOM, *n.* A room or apartment in the *forepart* of a house. BACKROOM, *n.* A room behind the *front room*, or in the *back part* of the house."—*Octavo Dict.* So of many phrases by which people tell of turning things, or changing the position of their parts; as, _in_side out, _out_side _in; up_side _down, down_side *up*; *wrong* end *foremost, but*-end *foremost*; *fore*-part *back, fore*-end *aft*; *hind* side _before, back_side *before*. Here all these contrasted particles seem to be adjectives of place or situation. What grammarians in general would choose to call them, it is hard to say; probably, many would satisfy themselves with calling the whole "*an adverbial phrase*,"—the common way of disposing of every thing which it is difficult to analyze. These, and the following examples from Scott, are a fair specimen of the uncertainty of present usage:

"The herds without a keeper strayed,
The plough was in *mid-furrow* staid."—*Lady of the Lake.*

"The eager huntsman knew his bound,
And in *mid chase* called off his hound."—*Ibidem.*

OBS. 3.—For the chief points of the compass, we have so many adjectives, and so many modes of varying or comparing them, that it is difficult to tell their number, or to know which to choose in practice. (1.) *North, south, east*, and *west*, are familiarly used both as nouns and as adjectives. From these it seems not improper to form superlatives, as above, by adding *most*; as, "From Aroar to Nebo, and the wild of *southmost* Abarim."—*Milton.* "There are no rivulets or springs in the island of Feror, the *westmost* of the Canaries."—*White's Nat. Hist.* (2.) These primitive terms may also be compared, in all three of the degrees, by the adverbs *farther* and *farthest,* or *further* and *furthest*; as, "Which is yet *farther west.*"—*Bacon.* (3.) Though we never employ as separate words the comparatives *norther, souther, easter, wester,* we have *northerly, southerly, easterly,* and *westerly*, which seem to have been formed from such comparatives, by adding *ly*; and these four may be compared by the adverbs *more* and *most,* or *less* and *least*: as, "These hills give us a view of the *most easterly, southerly,* and *westerly* parts of England."—GRAUNT: *in Joh. Dict.* (4.) From these supposed comparatives likewise, some authors form the superlatives *northermost, southermost, eastermost,* and *westermost*; as, "From the *westermost* part of Oyster bay."—*Dr. Webster's Hist. U. S.,* p. 126. "And three miles southward of the *southermost* part of said bay."—*Trumbull's Hist. of Amer.,* Vol. i, p. 88. "Pockanocket was on the *westermost* line of Plymouth Colony."—*Ib.,* p. 44. "As far as the *northermost* branch of the said bay or river."—*Ib.,* p. 127. The propriety of these is at least questionable; and, as they are neither very necessary to the language, nor recognized by any of our lexicographers, I forbear to approve them. (5.) From the four primitives we have also a third series of positives, ending in *ern*; as, *northern, southern, eastern, western.* These, though they have no comparatives of their own, not only form superlatives by assuming the termination *most,* but are sometimes compared, perhaps in both degrees, by a separate use of the adverbs: as, "*Southernmost, a.* Furthest towards the south."—*Webster's Dict.* "Until it shall intersect the *northernmost* part of the thirty-first degree of north latitude."—*Articles of Peace.* "To the *north-westernmost* head of Connecticut river."—*Ib.* "Thence through the said lake to the *most north-western* point thereof."—*Ib.*

OBS. 4.—It may be remarked of the comparatives *former* and *latter* or *hinder, upper* and *under* or *nether, inner* and *outer* or *utter, after* and *hither*; as well as of the Latin *superior* and *inferior, anterior* and *posterior, interior* and *exterior, prior* and *ulterior, senior* and *junior, major* and *minor*; that they cannot, like other comparatives, be construed with the conjunction *than.* After all genuine English comparatives, this conjunction may occur, because it is the only fit word for introducing the latter term of comparison; but we never say one thing is *former* or *latter, superior* or *inferior, than* an other. And so of all the rest here named. Again, no real comparative or superlative can ever need an other superadded to it; but *inferior* and *superior* convey ideas that do not always preclude the additional conception of *more* or *less*: as, "With respect to high and low notes, pronunciation is still *more inferior* to singing."—*Kames, Elements of Criticism*, Vol. ii, p. 73. "The mistakes which the *most superior* understanding is apt to fall into."—*West's Letters to a Young Lady*, p. 117.

OBS. 5.—Double comparatives and double superlatives, being in general awkward and unfashionable, as well as tautological, ought to be avoided. Examples: "The Duke of Milan, and his *more braver* daughter, could control thee."—*Shak., Tempest*. Say, "his *more gallant* daughter." "What in me was purchased, falls upon thee in a *more fairer* sort."—*Id., Henry IV.* Say, "*fairer*," or, "*more honest*;" for "*purchased*" here means *stolen*. "Changed to a *worser* shape thou canst not be."—*Id., Hen. VI.* Say, "a *worse* shape"—or, "an *uglier* shape." "After the *most straitest* sect of our religion, I lived a Pharisee."—*Acts*, xxvi, 5. Say, "the *strictest* sect." "Some say he's mad; others, that *lesser* hate him, do call it valiant fury."—*Shak.* Say, "others, that hate him *less*." In this last example, *lesser* is used adverbially; in which construction it is certainly incorrect. But against *lesser* as an adjective, some grammarians have spoken with more severity, than comports with a proper respect for authority. Dr. Johnson says, "LESSER, *adj*. A barbarous corruption of *less*, formed by the vulgar from the habit of terminating comparatives in *er; afterward adopted by poets, and then by writers of prose, till it has all the authority which a mode originally erroneous can derive from custom*."—*Quarto Dict.* With no great fairness, Churchill quotes this passage as far as the semicolon, and there stops. The position thus taken, he further endeavours to strengthen, by saying, "*Worser*, though *not more barbarous*, offends the ear in a much greater degree, because it has not been so frequently used."—*New Gram.*, p. 232. Example: "And God made two great lights; the greater light to rule the day, and the *lesser* light to rule the night."—*Gen.*, i, 16. Kirkham, after making an *imitation* of this passage, remarks upon it: "*Lesser* is *as incorrect as badder, gooder, worser*."—*Gram.*, p. 77. The judgement of any critic who is ignorant enough to say this, is worthy only of contempt. *Lesser* is still frequently used by the most tasteful authors, both in verse and prose: as, "It is the glowing style of a man who is negligent of *lesser* graces."—*Blair's Rhet.*, p. 189.

"Athos, Olympus, Ætna, Atlas, made
These hills seem things of *lesser* dignity."—*Byron*.

OBS. 6.—The adjective *little* is used in different senses; for it contrasts sometimes with *great*, and sometimes with *much*. *Lesser* appears to refer only to size. Hence *less* and *lesser* are not always equivalent terms. *Lesser* means *smaller*, and contrasts only with *greater*. *Less* contrasts sometimes with *greater*, but oftener with *more*, the comparative of *much*; for, though it may mean *not so large*, its most common meaning is *not so much*. It ought to be observed, likewise, that *less* is not an adjective of *number*,[182] though not unfrequently used as such. It does not mean *fewer*, and is therefore not properly employed in sentences like the following: "In all verbs, there are no *less* than three things implied at once."—*Blair's Rhet.*, p. 81. "*Smaller* things than three," is nonsense; and so, in reality, is what the Doctor here says. *Less* is not the proper opposite to *more*, when *more* is the comparative of *many: few, fewer, fewest*, are the only words which contrast regularly with *many, more, most*. In the following text, these comparatives are rightly employed: "And to the *more* ye shall give the *more* inheritance, and to the *fewer* ye shall give the *less* inheritance."—*Numbers*, xxxiii, 54. But if writers will continue to use *less* for *fewer*, so that "*less cattle*," for instance, may mean "*fewer cattle*;" we shall be under a sort of *necessity* to retain *lesser*, in order to speak intelligibly: as, "It shall be for the sending-forth of oxen, and for the treading of *lesser* cattle."—*Isaiah*, vii, 25. I have no partiality for the word *lesser*, neither will I make myself ridiculous by flouting at its rudeness. "This word," says Webster, "is a corruption, but [it is] too well established to be discarded. Authors always write the *Lesser*

Asia."—*Octavo Dict.* "By the same reason, may a man punish the *lesser* breaches of that law."—*Locke.* "When we speak of the *lesser* differences among the tastes of men."—*Blair's Rhet.*, p. 20. "In greater or *lesser* degrees of complexity."—*Burke, on Sublime*, p. 94. "The greater ought not to succumb to the *lesser*."—*Dillwyn's Reflections*, p. 128. "To such productions, *lesser* composers must resort for ideas."—*Gardiner's Music of Nature*, p. 413.

"The larger here, and there the *lesser* lambs,
The new-fall'n young herd bleating for their dams."—*Pope.*

OBS. 7.—Our grammarians deny the comparison of many adjectives, from a false notion that they are already superlatives. Thus W. Allen: "Adjectives compounded with the Latin preposition *per*, are already superlative: as, *perfect, perennial, permanent*, &c."—*Elements of E. Gram.*, p. 52. In reply to this, I would say, that nothing is really superlative, in English, but what has the form and construction of the superlative; as, "The *most permanent* of all dyes." No word beginning with *per*, is superlative by virtue of this Latin prefix. "Separate spirits, which are beings that have *perfecter* knowledge and greater happiness than we, must needs have also a *perfecter* way of communicating their thoughts than we have."—*Locke's Essay*, B. ii, Ch. 24, §36, This mode of comparison is not now good, but it shows that *perfect* is no superlative. Thus Kirkham: "The *following* adjectives, and *many others*, are *always in the superlative degree*; because, by expressing a quality *in the highest degree*, they carry in themselves a superlative signification: *chief, extreme, perfect, right, wrong, honest, just, true, correct, sincere, vast, immense, ceaseless, infinite, endless, unparalleled, universal, supreme, unlimited, omnipotent, all-wise, eternal.*" [183]—*Gram.*, p. 73. So the Rev. David Blair: "The words *perfect, certain, infinite, universal, chief, supreme, right, true, extreme, superior*, and some others, which express a perfect and superlative sense in themselves, do not admit of comparison."—*English Gram.*, p. 81. Now, according to Murray's definition, which Kirkham adopts, none of these words can be at all in the superlative degree. On the contrary, there are several among them, from which true superlatives are frequently and correctly formed. Where are the positives which are here supposed to be "*increased to the highest degree?*" Every real superlative in our language, except *best* and *worst, most* and *least, first* and *last,* with the still more irregular word *next,* is a derivative, formed from some other English word, by adding *est* or *most*; as, *truest, hindmost.* The propriety or impropriety of comparing the foregoing words, or any of the "*many others*" of which this author speaks, is to be determined according to their meaning, and according to the usage of good writers, and not by the dictation of a feeble pedant, or upon the supposition that if compared they would form "*double superlatives.*"

OBS. 8.—*Chief* is from the French word *chef,* the *head: chiefest* is therefore no more a double superlative than *headmost*: "But when the *headmost* foes appeared."—*Scott.* Nor are *chief* and *chiefest* equivalent terms: "Doeg an Edomite, the *chiefest* of the herdsmen."—*1 Samuel,* xxi, 7. "The *chief* of the herdsmen," would convey a different meaning; it would be either the *leader* of the herdsmen, or the *principal part* of them. *Chiefest,* however, has often been used where *chief* would have been better; as, "He sometimes denied admission to the *chiefest* officers of the army."— *Clarendon,* let us look further at Kirkham's list of *absolute* "*superlatives.*"

OBS. 9.—*Extreme* is from the Latin superlative *extremus,* and of course its literal signification is not really susceptible of increase. Yet *extremest* has been used, and is still used, by some of the very best writers; as, "They thought it the *extremest* of evils."—*Bacon.* "That on the sea's *extremest* border stood."—*Addison.* "How, to *extremest* thrill of agony."—*Pollok,* B. viii, l. 270. "I go th' *extremest* remedy to prove."—*Dryden.* "In *extremest* poverty."—*Swift.* "The hairy fool stood on th' *extremest* verge of the swift brook, augmenting it with tears."—*Shak.* "While the *extremest* parts of the earth were meditating submission."—*Atterbury.* "His writings are poetical to the *extremest* boundaries of poetry."—*Adams's Rhetoric*, i, 87. In prose, this superlative is not now very common; but the poets still occasionally use it, for the sake of their measure; and it ought to be noticed that the simple adjective is *not partitive.* If we say, for the first example, "the *extreme* of evils;" we make the word a *noun*, and do not convey exactly the same idea that is there expressed.

OBS. 10.—*Perfect*, if taken in its strictest sense, must not be compared; but this word, like many others which mean most in the positive, is often used with a certain latitude of meaning, which renders its comparison by the adverbs not altogether inadmissible; nor is it destitute of authority, as I have already shown. (See Obs. 8th, p. 280.) "From the first rough sketches, to the *more perfect* draughts."—*Bolingbroke, on Hist.*, p. 152. "The *most perfect*."—*Adams's Lect. on Rhet.*, i, 99 and 136; ii, 17 and 57: *Blair's Lect.*, pp. 20 and 399. "The most *beautiful and perfect* example of analysis."—*Lowth's Gram., Pref.*, p. 10. "The plainest, *most perfect*, and most useful manual."—*Bullions's E. Gram., Rev.*, p. 7. "Our sight is the *most perfect*, and the most delightful, of all our senses."—*Addison, Spect.*, No. 411; *Blair's Lect.*, pp. 115 and 194; *Murray's Gram.*, i, 322. Here Murray anonymously copied Blair. "And to render natives *more perfect* in the knowledge of it."—*Campbell's Rhet.*, p. 171; *Murray's Gram.*, p. 366. Here Murray copied Campbell, the most accurate of all his masters. Whom did he copy when he said, "The phrases, *more perfect*, and *most perfect*, are improper?"—*Octavo Gram.*, p. 168. But if these are wrong, so is the following sentence: "No poet has ever attained a *greater perfection* than Horace."—*Blair's Lect.*, p. 398. And also this: "Why are we brought into the world *less perfect* in respect to our nature?"—*West's Letters to a Young Lady*, p. 220.

OBS. 11.—*Right* and *wrong* are not often compared by good writers; though we sometimes see such phrases as *more right* and *more wrong*, and such words as *rightest* and *wrongest*: "'Tis always in the *wrongest* sense."— *Butler*. "A method of attaining the *rightest* and greatest happiness."— PRICE: *Priestley's Gram.*, p. 78. "It is no *more right* to steal apples, than it is to steal money."—*Webster's New Spelling-Book*, p. 118. There are equivalent expressions which seem preferable; as, *more proper, more erroneous, most proper, most erroneous.*

OBS. 12.—*Honest, just, true, correct, sincere,* and *vast,* may all be compared at pleasure. Pope's Essay on Criticism is *more correct* than any thing this modest pretender can write; and in it, he may find the comparative *juster*, the superlatives *justest, truest, sincerest,* and the phrases, "*So vast* a throng,"—"*So vast* is art:" all of which are contrary to his teaching. "*Unjuster* dealing is used in buying than in selling."—*Butler's Poems*, p. 163. "*Iniquissimam* pacem *justissimo* bello antefero."—*Cicero*. "I prefer the *unjustest* peace before the *justest* war."—*Walker's English Particles*, p. 68. The poet Cowley used the word *honestest*; which is not now very common. So Swift: "What *honester* folks never durst for their ears."—*The Yahoo's Overthrow*. So Jucius: "The *honestest* and ablest men."—*Letter XVIII*. "The sentence would be *more correct* in the following form."—*Murray's Gram.*, i, p. 223. "Elegance is chiefly gained by studying the *correctest* writers."—*Holmes's Rhetoric*, p. 27. *Honest* and *correct*, for the sake of euphony, require the adverbs; as, *more honest*, "*most correct*."— *Lowth's Gram., Pref.*, p. iv. *Vast, vaster, vastest*, are words as smooth, as *fast, faster, fastest*; and *more vast* is certainly as good English as *more just*: "Shall mortal man be *more just* than God?"—*Job*, iv, 17. "Wilt thou condemn him that is *most just*?"—*Ib.*, xxxiv, 17. "More wise, more learn'd, *more just*, more-everything."—*Pope*. *Universal* is often compared by the adverbs, but certainly with no reënforcement of meaning: as, "One of the *most universal* precepts, is, that the orator himself should feel the passion."—*Adams's Rhet.*, i, 379. "Though not *so universal.*"—*Ib.*, ii, 311. "This experience is general, though not *so universal*, as the absence of memory in childhood."—*Ib.*, ii, 362. "We can suppose no motive which would *more universally* operate."—*Dr. Blair's Rhet.*, p. 55. "Music is known to have been *more universally* studied."—*Ib.*, p. 123. "We shall not wonder, that his grammar has been *so universally* applauded."—*Walker's Recommendation in Murray's Gram.*, ii, 306. "The pronoun *it* is the *most universal* of all the pronouns."—*Cutler's Gram.*, p. 66. Thus much for one half of this critic's twenty-two "*superlatives.*" The rest are simply adjectives that are not susceptible of comparison: they are not "superlatives" at all. A man might just as well teach, that *good* is a superlative, and not susceptible of comparison, because "*there is none good but one.*"

OBS. 13.—Pronominal adjectives, when their nouns are expressed, simply relate to them, and have no modifications: except *this* and *that*, which form the plurals *these* and *those*; and *much, many*, and a few others, which are compared. Examples: "Whence hath *this* man *this* wisdom, and *these* mighty works?"—*Matt.*, xiii, 54. "But *some* man will say, How are the dead raised up? and with *what* body do they come?"—*1 Cor.*, xv, 35. "The *first* man Adam was made a living soul; the *last* Adam was made a quickening spirit."—*Ib.*, 45. So, when one pronominal adjective "precedes an other, the former *must be taken* simply as an adjective;" as,

"Those suns are set. O rise *some other* such!" —*Cowper's Task*, B. ii, l. 252.

OBS. 14.—Pronominal adjectives, when their nouns are not expressed, may be parsed as representing them in *person, number, gender*, and *case*; but those who prefer it, may supply the ellipsis, and parse the adjective, *simply as an adjective*. Example: "He threatens *many*, who injures *one*."—*Kames*. Here it may be said, "*Many* is a pronominal adjective, meaning *many persons*; of the third person, plural number, masculine gender, and objective case." Or those who will take the word simply as an adjective, may say, "*Many* is a pronominal adjective, of the positive degree, compared *many, more, most*, and relating to *persons* understood." And so of "*one*," which represents, or relates to, *person* understood. Either say, "*One* is a pronominal adjective, not compared," and give the *three definitions* accordingly; or else say, "One is a pronominal adjective, relating to *person* understood; of the third person, singular number, masculine gender, and objective case," and give the *six definitions* accordingly.

OBS. 15.—*Elder* for *older*, and *eldest* for *oldest*, are still frequently used; though the ancient positive, *eld* for *old*, is now obsolete. Hence some have represented *old* as having a two-fold comparison; and have placed it, not very properly, among the irregular adjectives. The comparatives *elder* and *better*, are often used as *nouns*; so are the Latin comparatives *superior* and *inferior, interior* and *exterior, senior* and *junior, major* and *minor*: as, The *elder's* advice,—One of the *elders*,—His *betters*,—Our *superiors*,—The *interior* of the country,—A handsome *exterior*,—Your *seniors*,—My *juniors*,—A *major* in the army,—He is yet a *minor*. The word *other*, which has something of the nature of a comparative, likewise takes the form of a noun, as before suggested; and, in that form, the reader, if he will, may call it a noun: as, "What do ye more than *others*?"—*Bible*. "God in thus much is bounded, that the evil hath he left unto *an other*; and *that Dark Other* hath usurped the evil which Omnipotence laid down."—*Tupper's Book of Thoughts*, p. 45. Some call it a pronoun. But it seems to be pronominal, merely by ellipsis of the noun after it; although, unlike a mere adjective, it assumes the ending of the noun, to mark that ellipsis. Perhaps therefore, the best explanation of it would be this: "'*Others* is a pronominal adjective, having the form of a noun, and put for *other men*; in the third person, plural number, masculine gender, and nominative case." The gender of this word varies, according to that of the contrasted term; and the case, according to the relation it bears to other words. In the following example, it is neuter and objective: "The fibres of this muscle act as those of *others*."—*Cheyne*. Here, "as *those of others*," means, "as *the fibres* of *other muscles*."

OBS. 16.—"Comparatives and superlatives seem sometimes to part with their relative nature, and only to retain their *intensive*, especially those which are formed by the superlative adverb *most*; as, 'A *most learned* man,'—'A *most brave* man:' i. e. not the bravest or the most learned man that ever was, but a man possessing bravery or learning in a very eminent degree."—See *Alexander Murray's Gram.*, p. 110. This use of the terms of comparison is thought by some not to be very grammatical.

OBS. 17.—Contractions of the superlative termination *est*, as *high'st* for *highest, bigg'st for biggest*, though sometimes used by the poets, are always inelegant, and may justly be considered grammatically improper. They occur most frequently in doggerel verse, like that of *Hudibras*; the author of which work, wrote, in his droll fashion, not only the foregoing monosyllables, but *learned'st* for *most learned, activ'st* for *most active, desperat'st* for *most desperate, epidemical'st* for *most epidemical*, &c.

"And *th' activ'st* fancies share as loose alloys,
For want of equal weight to counterpoise."—*Butler's Poems.*

"Who therefore finds the *artificial'st* fools
Have not been chang'd *i th'* cradle, but the schools."—*Ib.*, p. 143.

OBS. 18.—Nouns used adjectively are not varied in number to agree with the nouns to which they relate, but what is singular or plural when used substantively, is without number when taken as an adjective: as, "One of the nine *sister* goddesses."—*Webster's Dict., w. Muse.* "He has money in a *savings* bank." The latter mode of expression is uncommon, and the term *savings-bank* is sometimes compounded, but the hyphen does not really affect the nature of the former word. It is doubtful, however, whether a plural noun can ever properly assume the character of an adjective; because, if it is not then really the same as the possessive case, it will always be liable to be thought a false form of that case. What Johnson wrote "*fullers earth*" and "*fullers thistle*;" Chalmers has "*fullers earth*" and "*fuller's thistle*;" Webster, "*fuller's-earth*" and "*fuller's-thistle*;" Ainsworth, "*fuller's earth*" and "*fuller's thistle*;" Walker has only "*fullers-earth*;" Worcester, "*fuller's-earth*;" Cobb, "*fullers earth*;" the Treasury of Knowledge, "*fullers'-earth*." So unsettled is this part of our grammar, that in many such cases it is difficult cult to say whether we ought to use the apostrophe, or the hyphen, or both, or neither. To insert neither, unless we make a close compound, is to use a plural noun adjectively; which form, I think, is the most objectionable of all. See "*All souls day*,"—"*All-fools-day*,"—"*All-saints'-day*," &c., in the dictionaries. These may well be written "*All Souls' Day*" &c.

EXAMPLES FOR PARSING.

PRAXIS IV.—ETYMOLOGICAL.

In the Fourth Praxis, it is required of the pupil—to distinguish and define the different parts of speech, and the classes and modifications of the ARTICLES, NOUNS, *and* ADJECTIVES.

The definitions to be given in the Fourth Praxis, are two for an article, six for a noun, three for an adjective, and one for a pronoun, a verb, a participle, an adverb, a conjunction, a preposition, or an interjection. Thus: —

EXAMPLE PARSED.

"The best and most effectual method of teaching grammar, is precisely that of which the careless are least fond: teach learnedly, rebuking whatsoever is false, blundering, or unmannerly."—*G. Brown.*

The is the definite article. 1. An article is the word *the, an,* or *a,* which we put before nouns to limit their signification. 2. The definite article is *the,* which denotes some particular thing or things.

Best is a common adjective, of the superlative degree; compared irregularly, *good, better, best.* 1. An adjective is a word added to a noun or pronoun, and generally expresses quality. 2. A common adjective is any ordinary epithet, or adjective denoting quality or situation. 3. The superlative degree is that which is *most* or *least* of all included with it.

And, is a conjunction. 1. A conjunction is a word used to connect words or sentences in constructing, and to show the dependence of the terms so connected.

Most is an adverb. 1. An adverb is a word added to a verb, a participle, an adjective, or an other adverb; and generally expresses time, place, degree, or manner.

Effectual is a common adjective, compared by means of the adverbs; *effectual, more effectual, most effectual*; or, *effectual, less effectual, least effectual.* 1. An adjective is a word added to a noun or pronoun, and generally expresses quality. 2. A common adjective is any ordinary epithet, or adjective denoting quality or situation. 3. Those adjectives which may be varied in sense, but not in form, are compared by means of adverbs.

Method is a common noun, of the third person, singular number, neuter gender, and nominative case. 1. A noun is the name of any person, place, or thing, that can be known or mentioned. 2. A common noun is the name of a sort, kind, or class, of beings or things. 3. The third person, is that which denotes the person or thing merely spoken of. 4. The singular number is that which denotes but one. 5. The neuter gender is that which denotes things that are neither male nor female. 6. The nominative case is that form or state of a noun or pronoun, which usually denotes the subject of a finite verb.

Of is a preposition. 1. A preposition is a word used to express some relation of different things or thoughts to each other, and is generally placed before a noun or a pronoun.

Teaching is a participle. 1. A participle is a word derived from a verb, participating the properties of a verb, and of an adjective or a noun; and is generally formed by adding *ing, d,* or *ed,* to the verb.

Grammar is a common noun, of the third person, singular number, neuter gender, and objective case. 1. A noun is the name of any person, place or thing, that can be known or mentioned. 2. A common noun is the name of a sort, kind, or class, of beings or things. 3. The third person is that which denotes the person or thing merely spoken of. 4. The singular number is that which denotes but one. 5. The neuter gender is that which denotes things that are neither male nor female. 6. The objective case is that form or state of a noun or pronoun, which usually denotes the object of a verb, participle, or preposition.

Is is a verb. 1. A verb is a word that signifies *to be, to act,* or *to be acted upon.*

Precisely is an adverb. 1. An adverb is a word added to a verb, a participle, an adjective, or an other adverb; and generally expresses time, place, degree, or manner.

That is a pronominal adjective, not compared; standing for *that method*, in the third person, singular number, neuter gender, and nominative case. [See OBS. 14th,] 1. An adjective is a word added to a noun or pronoun, and generally expresses quality. 2. A pronominal adjective is a definitive word which may either accompany its noun or represent it understood. 3. The third person is that which denotes the person or thing merely spoken of. 4. The singular number is that which denotes but one. 5. The neuter gender is that which denotes things that are neither male nor female. 6. The nominative case is that form or state of a noun or pronoun, which usually denotes the subject of a finite verb.

Of is a preposition. 1. A preposition is a word used to express some relation of different things or thoughts to each other, and is generally placed before a noun or a pronoun.

Which is a pronoun. 1. A pronoun is a word used in stead of a noun.

The is the definite article. 1. An article is the word *the, an,* or *a,* which we put before nouns to limit their signification. 2. The definite article is *the,* which denotes some particular thing or things.

Careless is a common adjective, compared by means of the adverbs; *careless, more careless, most careless;* or, *careless, less careless, least careless.* 1. An adjective is a word added to a noun or pronoun, and generally expresses quality. 2. A common adjective is any ordinary epithet, or adjective denoting quality or situation. 3. Those adjectives which may be varied in sense, but not in form, are compared by means of adverbs.

Are is a verb. 1. A verb is a word that signifies *to be, to act,* or *to be acted upon.*

Least is an adverb. 1. An adverb is a word added to a verb, a participle, an adjective, or an other adverb; and generally expresses time, place, degree, or manner.

Fond is a common adjective, compared regularly, *fond, fonder, fondest*; but here made superlative by the adverb *least*. 1. An adjective is a word added to a noun or pronoun, and generally expresses quality. 2. A common adjective is any ordinary epithet, or adjective denoting quality or situation. 8. The superlative degree is that which is *most* or *least* of all included with it.

Teach is a verb. 1. A verb is a word that signifies *to be, to act*, or *to be acted upon*.

Learnedly is an adverb. 1. An adverb is a word added to a verb, a participle, an adjective, or an other adverb; and generally expresses time, place, degree, or manner.

Rebuking is a participle. 1. A participle is a word derived from a verb, participating the properties of a verb, and of an adjective or a noun; and is generally formed by adding *ing, d,* or *ed*, to the verb.

Whatsoever is a pronoun. 1. A pronoun is a word used in stead of a noun.

Is is a verb. 1. A verb is a word that signifies *to be, to act*, or *to be acted upon*.

False is a common adjective, of the positive degree; compared regularly, *false, falser, falsest*. 1. An adjective is a word added to a noun or pronoun, and generally expresses quality. 2. A common adjective is any ordinary epithet, or adjective denoting quality or situation. 3. The positive degree is that which is expressed by the adjective in its simple form.

Blundering is a participial adjective, compared by means of the adverbs; *blundering, more blundering, most blundering*; or, *blundering, less blundering, least blundering*. 1. An adjective is a word added to a noun or pronoun, and generally expresses quality. 2. A participial adjective is one that has the form of a participle, but differs from it by rejecting the idea of time. 3. Those adjectives which may be varied in sense, but not in form, are compared by means of adverbs.

Or is a conjunction. 1. A conjunction is a word used to connect words or sentences in construction, and to show the dependence of the terms so connected.

Unmannerly is a common adjective, compared by means of the adverbs; *unmannerly, more unmannerly, most unmannerly*; or, *unmannerly, less unmannerly, least unmannerly*. 1. An adjective is a word added to a noun or pronoun, and generally expresses quality. 2. A common adjective is any ordinary epithet, or adjective denoting quality or situation. 3. Those adjectives which may be varied in sense, but not in form, are compared by means of adverbs.

LESSON I.—PARSING.

"The noblest and most beneficial invention of which human ingenuity can boast, is that of writing."—*Robertson's America*, Vol. II, p. 193.

"Charlemagne was the tallest, the handsomest, and the strongest man of his time; his appearance was truly majestic, and he had surprising agility in all sorts of manly exercises."—*Stories of France*, p. 19.

"Money, like other things, is more or less valuable, as it is less or more plentiful."—*Beanie's Moral Science*, p. 378.

"The right way of acting, is, in a moral sense, as much a reality, in the mind of an ordinary man, as the straight or the right road."—*Dr. Murray's Hist. Lang.*, i, 118.

"The full period of several members possesses most dignity and modulation, and conveys also the greatest degree of force, by admitting the closest compression of thought."—*Jamieson's Rhet.*, p. 79.

"His great master, Demosthenes, in addressing popular audiences, never had recourse to a similar expedient. He avoided redundancies, as equivocal and feeble. He aimed only to make the deepest and most efficient impression; and he employed for this purpose, the plainest, the fewest, and the most emphatic words."—*Ib.*, p. 68.

"The high eloquence which I have last mentioned, is always the offspring of passion. A man actuated by a strong passion, becomes much greater than he is at other times. He is conscious of more strength and force; he utters greater sentiments, conceives higher designs, and executes them with a boldness and felicity, of which, on other occasions, he could not think himself capable."—*Blair's Rhet.*, p. 236.

"His words bore sterling weight, nervous and strong,
In manly tides of sense they roll'd along."—*Churchill*.

"To make the humble proud, the proud submiss,
Wiser the wisest, and the brave more brave."—*W. S. Landor*.

LESSON II.—PARSING.

"I am satisfied that in this, as in all cases, it is best, safest, as well as most right and honorable, to speak freely and plainly."—*Channing's Letter to Clay*, p. 4.

"The gospel, when preached with the Holy Ghost sent down from heaven, through the wonder-working power of God, can make the proud humble, the selfish disinterested, the worldly heavenly, the sensual pure."—*Christian Experience*, p. 399.

"I am so much the better, as I am the liker[184] the best; and so much the holier, as I am more conformable to the holiest, or rather to Him who is holiness itself."—*Bp. Beneridge*.

"Whether any thing in Christianity appears to them probable, or improbable; consistent, or inconsistent; agreeable to what they should have expected, or the contrary; wise and good, or ridiculous and useless; is perfectly irrelevant."—*M'Ilvaine's Evidences*, p. 523.

"God's providence is higher, and deeper, and larger, and stronger, than all the skill of his adversaries; and his pleasure shall be accomplished in their overthrow, except they repent and become his friends."—*Cox, on Christianity*, p. 445.

"A just relish of what is beautiful, proper, elegant, and ornamental, in writing or painting, in architecture or gardening, is a fine preparation for the same just relish of these qualities in character and behaviour. To the man who has acquired a taste so acute and accomplished, every action wrong or improper must be highly disgustful: if, in any instance, the overbearing power of passion sway him from his duty, he returns to it with redoubled resolution never to be swayed a second time."—*Kames, Elements of Criticism*, Vol. i, p. 25.

"In grave Quintilian's copious work, we find
The justest rules and clearest method join'd."—*Pope, on Crit.*

LESSON III.—PARSING.

"There are several sorts of scandalous tempers; some malicious, and some effeminate; others obstinate, brutish, and savage. Some humours are childish and silly; some, false, and others, scurrilous; some, mercenary, and some, tyrannical."—*Collier's Antoninus*, p. 52.

"Words are obviously voluntary signs: and they are also arbitrary; excepting a few simple sounds expressive of certain internal emotions, which sounds being the same in all languages, must be the work of nature: thus the unpremeditated tones of admiration are the same in all men."—*Kames, Elements of Crit.*, i, 347.

"A stately and majestic air requires sumptuous apparel, which ought not to be gaudy, nor crowded with little ornaments. A woman of consummate beauty can bear to be highly adorned, and yet shows best in a plain dress."—*Ib.*, p. 279. "Of all external objects a graceful person is the most agreeable. But in vain will a person attempt to be graceful, who is deficient in amiable qualities."—*Ib.*, p. 299.

"The faults of a writer of acknowledged excellence are more dangerous, because the influence of his example is more extensive; and the interest of learning requires that they should be discovered and stigmatized, before they have the sanction of antiquity bestowed upon them, and become precedents of indisputable authority."—*Dr. Johnson, Rambler*, Vol. ii, No. 93.

"Judges ought to be more learned than witty, more reverend than plausible, and more advised than confident; above all things, integrity is their portion and proper virtue."—*Bacon's Essays*, p. 145.

"The wisest nations, having the most and best ideas, will consequently have the best and most copious languages."—*Harris's Hermes*, p. 408.

"Here we trace the operation of powerful causes, while we remain ignorant of their nature; but everything goes on with such regularity and harmony, as to give a striking and convincing proof of a combining directing intelligence."—*Life of W. Allen*, Vol. i, p. 170.

"The wisest, unexperienced, will be ever
Timorous and loth, with novice modesty,
Irresolute, unhardy, unadventurous."—*Milton.*

IMPROPRIETIES FOR CORRECTION.

ERRORS OF ADJECTIVES.

LESSON I.—DEGREES.

"I have the real excuse of the honestest sort of bankrupts."—*Cowley's Preface*, p. viii.

[FORMULE.—Not proper, because the adjective *honestest* is harshly compared by *est*. But, according to a principle stated on page 283d concerning the regular degrees, "This method of comparison is to be applied only to monosyllables, and to dissyllables of a smooth termination, or such as receive it and still have but one syllable after the accent." Therefore, *honestest* should be *most honest*; thus, "I have real excuse of the *most honest* sort of bankrupts."]

"The honourablest part of talk, is, to give the occasion."—*Bacon's Essays*, p. 90. "To give him one of his own modestest proverbs."—*Barclay's Works*, iii, 340. "Our language is now certainly properer and more natural, than it was formerly."—*Bp. Burnet.* "Which will be of most and frequentest use to him in the world."—*Locke, on Education*, p. 163. "The same is notified in the notablest places in the diocese."—*Whitgift.* "But it was the dreadfullest sight that ever I saw."—*Pilgrim's Progress*, p. 70. "Four of the ancientest, soberest, and discreetest of the brethren, chosen for the occasion, shall regulate it."—*Locke, on Church Gov*. "Nor can there be any clear understanding of any Roman author, especially of ancienter time, without this skill."—*Walker's Particles*, p. x. "Far the learnedest of the Greeks."—*Ib.*, p. 120. "The learneder thou art, the humbler be thou."—*Ib.*, p. 228. "He is none of the best or honestest."— *Ib.*, p. 274. "The properest methods of communicating it to others."— *Burn's Gram.*, Prof, p. viii. "What heaven's great King hath powerfullest to send against us."—*Paradise Lost*. "Benedict is not the unhopefullest husband that I know."—SHAK.: *in Joh. Dict.* "That he should immediately do all the meanest and triflingest things himself."—RAY: *in Johnson's Gram.*, p. 6. "I shall be named among the famousest of women."—MILTON'S *Samson Agonistes: ib.* "Those have the inventivest heads for all purposes."—ASCHAM: *ib.* "The wretcheder are the contemners of all helps."—BEN JONSON: *ib.* "I will now deliver a few of the properest and naturallest considerations that belong to this piece."—WOTTON: *ib.* "The mortalest poisons practised by the West Indians, have some mixture of the blood, fat, or flesh of man."—BACON: *ib.* "He so won upon him, that he rendered him one of the faithfulest and most affectionate allies the Medes ever had."—*Rollin*, ii, 71. "'You see before you,' says he to him, 'the most devoted servant, and the faithfullest ally, you ever had.'"—*Ib.*, ii, 79. "I chose the flourishing'st tree in all the park."—*Cowley*. "Which he placed, I think, some centuries backwarder than Julius Africanus thought fit to place it afterwards."—*Bolingbroke, on History*, p. 53. "The Tiber, the notedest river of Italy."—*Littleton's Dict.*

"To fartherest shores the ambrosial spirit flies."
—*Cutler's Gram.*, p. 140.

——"That what she wills to do or say,

Seems wisest, virtuousest, discreetest, best."

—*Milton,* B. viii, l. 550.

LESSON II.—MIXED.

"During the three or four first years of its existence."—*Taylor's District School*, p. 27.

[FORMULE.—Not proper, because the cardinal numbers, *three* and *four* are put before the ordinal *first*. But, according to the 7th part of Obs. 7th, page 280th, "In specifying any part of a series, we ought to place the cardinal number after the ordinal." Therefore the words *three* and *four* should be placed after *first*; thus, "During the *first three* or *four* years of its existence."]

"To the first of these divisions, my ten last lectures have been devoted."—*Adams's Rhet.*, Vol. i, p. 391. "There are in the twenty-four states not less than sixty thousand common schools."—*Taylor's District School*, p. 38. "I know of nothing which gives teachers so much trouble as this want of firmness."—*Ib.*, p. 57. "I know of nothing that throws such darkness over the line which separates right from wrong."—*Ib.*, p. 58. "None need this purity and simplicity of language and thought so much as the common school instructor."—*Ib.*, p. 64. "I know of no periodical that is so valuable to the teacher as the Annals of Education."—*Ib.*, p. 67. "Are not these schools of the highest importance? Should not every individual feel the deepest interest in their character and condition?"—*Ib.*, p. 78. "If instruction were made a profession, teachers would feel a sympathy for each other."—*Ib.*, p. 93. "Nothing is so likely to interest children as novelty and change."—*Ib.*, p. 131. "I know of no labour which affords so much happiness as that of the teacher's."—*Ib.*, p. 136. "Their school exercises are the most pleasant and agreeable of any that they engage in."—*Ib.*, p. 136. "I know of no exercise so beneficial to the pupil as that of drawing maps."—*Ib.*, p. 176. "I know of nothing in which our district schools are so defective as they are in the art of teaching grammar."—*Ib.*, p. 196. "I know of nothing so easily acquired as history."—*Ib.* p. 206. "I know of nothing for which scholars usually have such an abhorrence, as composition."—*Ib.*, p. 210. "There is nothing in our fellow-men that we should respect with so much sacredness as their good name."—*Ib.*, p. 307. "Sure never any thing was so unbred as that odious man."—CONGREVE: *in Joh. Dict.* "In the dialogue between the mariner and the shade of the deceast."—*Philological Museum*, i, 466. "These master-works would still be less excellent and finisht"—*Ib.*, i, 469. "Every attempt to staylace the language of polisht conversation, renders our phraseology inelegant and clumsy."—*Ib.*, i, 678. "Here are a few of the unpleasant'st words that ever blotted paper."—SHAK.: *in Joh. Dict.* "With the most easy, undisobliging transitions."—BROOME: *ib.* "Fear is, of all affections, the unaptest to admit any conference with reason."—HOOKER: *ib.* "Most chymists think glass a body more undestroyable than gold itself."—BOYLE: *ib.* "To part with unhackt edges, and bear back our barge undinted."—SHAK.: *ib.* "Erasmus, who was an unbigotted Roman Catholic, was transported with this passage."—ADDISON: *ib.* "There are no less than five words, with any of which the sentence might have terminated."—*Campbell's Rhet.*, p. 397. "The one preach Christ of contention; but the other, of love."—*Philippians*, i, 16. "Hence we find less discontent and heart-burnings, than where the subjects are unequally burdened."—*Art of Thinking*, p. 56.

"The serpent, subtil'st beast of all the field,
I knew; but not with human voice indu'd."
—MILTON: *Joh. Dict., w. Human.*

"How much more grievous would our lives appear,
  To reach th' eighth hundred, than the eightieth year?"
    —DENHAM: B. P., ii, 244.

LESSON III.—MIXED.

"Brutus engaged with Aruns; and so fierce was the attack, that they pierced one another at the same time."—*Lempriere's Dict.*

[FORMULE.—Not proper, because the phrase *one another* is here applied to two persons only, the words *an* and *other* being needlessly compounded. But, according to Observation 15th, on the Classes of Adjectives, *each other* must be applied to two persons or things, and *one an other* to more than two. Therefore *one another* should here be *each other*; thus, "Brutus engaged with Aruns; and so fierce was the attack, that they pierced *each other* at the same time."]

"Her two brothers were one after another turned into stone."—*Art of Thinking*, p. 194. "Nouns are often used as adjectives; as, A *gold*-ring, a *silver*-cup."—*Lennie's Gram.*, p. 14. "Fire and water destroy one another."—*Wanostrocht's Gram.*, p. 82. "Two negatives in English destroy one another, or are equivalent to an affirmative."—*Lowth's Gram.*, p. 94; *E. Devis's*, 111; *Mack's*, 147; *Murray's*, 198; *Churchill's*, 148; *Putnam's*, 135; *C. Adams's*, 102; *Hamlin's*, 79; *Alger's*, 66; *Fisk's*, 140; *Ingersoll's*, 207; and *many others*. "Two negatives destroy one another, and are generally equivalent to an affirmative."—*Kirkham's Gram.*, p. 191; *Felton's*, 85. "Two negatives destroy one another and make an affirmative."—*J. Flint's Gram.*, p. 79. "Two negatives destroy one another, being equivalent to an affirmative."—*Frost's El. of E. Gram.*, p. 48. "Two objects, resembling one another, are presented to the imagination."—*Parker's Exercises in Comp.*, p. 47. "Mankind, in order to hold converse with each other, found it necessary to give names to objects."—*Kirkham's Gram.*, p. 42. "Words are derived from each other[185] in various ways."—*Cooper's Gram.*, p. 108. "There are many other ways of deriving words from one another."—*Murray's Gram.*, p. 131. "When several verbs connected by conjunctions, succeed each other in a sentence, the auxiliary is usually omitted except with the first."—*Frost's Gram.*, p. 91. "Two or more verbs, having the same nominative case, and immediately following one another, are also separated by commas." [186]—*Murray's Gram.*, p. 270; *C. Adams's*, 126; *Russell's*, 113; and others. "Two or more adverbs immediately succeeding each other, must be separated by commas."—*Same Grammars.* "If, however, the members succeeding each other, are very closely connected, the comma is unnecessary."—*Murray's Gram.*, p. 273; *Comly's*, 152; *and others.* "Gratitude, when exerted towards one another, naturally produces a very pleasing sensation in the mind of a grateful man."—*Mur.*, p. 287. "Several verbs in the infinitive mood, having a common dependence, and succeeding one another, are also divided by commas."—*Comly's Gram.*, p. 153. "The several words of which it consists, have so near a relation to each other."—*Murray's Gram.*, p. 268; *Comly's*, 144; *Russell's*, 111; *and others.* "When two or more verbs have the same nominative, and immediately follow one another, or two or more adverbs immediately succeed one another, they must be separated by commas."—*Comly's Gram.*, p. 145. "Nouns frequently succeed each other, meaning the same thing."—*Sanborn's Gram.*, p. 63. "And these two tenses may thus answer one another."—*Johnson's Gram. Com.*, p. 322. "Or some other relation which two objects bear to one another."—*Jamieson's Rhet.*, p. 149. "That the heathens tolerated each other, is allowed."—*Gospel its own Witness*, p. 76. "And yet these two persons love one another tenderly."—*Murray's E. Reader*, p. 112. "In the six hundredth and first year."—*Gen.*, viii, 13. "Nor is this arguing of his but a reiterate clamour."—*Barclay's Works*, i, 250. "In severals of them the inward life of Christianity is to be found."—*Ib.*, iii, 272. "Though

Alvarez, Despauterius, and other, allow it not to be Plural."—*Johnson's Gram. Com.*, p. 169. "Even the most dissipate and shameless blushed at the sight."—*Lemp. Dict., w. Antiochus.* "We feel a superior satisfaction in surveying the life of animals, than that of vegetables."—*Jamieson's Rhet.*, 172. "But this man is so full fraughted with malice."—*Barclay's Works*, i11, 205. "That I suggest some things concerning the properest means."—*Blair's Rhet.*, p. 337.